Beginner Landlord

101 Forms to Managing Rental Property Investing

Legal Self-Help Guide

Beginner Landlord

101 Forms to Managing Rental Property Investing

Legal Self-Help Guide

Sanket Mistry, Esq., J.D., M.I.A.

Nikita Mistry, Esq., LL.M., LL.B.

Peerless Legal

ISBN 13: 978-1-940788-16-6
ISBN 10: 1-940788-16-1
Library of Congress Control Number: 2020900525

Mistry, Sanket and Mistry, Nikita
Beginner Landlord: 101 Forms to Managing Rental Property Investing, Legal Self-Help Guide
First Edition
Peerless Legal | Roanoke, Virginia | www.PeerlessLegal.com

™ and Peerless Legal are trademarks of PeerlessLegal.com.

Peerless Legal books are available for special promotions. For details, contact Peerless Legal by email at sales@peerlesslegal.com, or visit www.PeerlessLegal.com.

While the author has made every effort to provide accurate telephone numbers and Internet addresses at the time of publication, neither the publisher nor author assume any responsibility for errors or changes that occur after publication. The publisher does not have any control over, and does not assume any responsibility for, author or third-party websites or their content.

This publication is designed to provide accurate and authoritative information in regard to the subject matters covered. It is sold with the understanding that the publisher and author are not engaged in rendering legal, accounting, or other professional services. If legal advice or other expert assistance is required, the services of a competent professional should be sought.

From a *Declaration of Principles jointly adopted by a Committee of the American Bar Association and a Committee of Publishers*

THIS PRODUCT IS NOT A SUBSTITUTE FOR LEGAL ADVICE.
Disclaimer required by Texas statutes.

DISCLAIMER

Laws change constantly. Every effort has been made to provide the most up-to-date information. However, the author, publisher, and any and all persons or entities involved in any way in the preparation, publication, sale, or distribution of this publication disclaim any and all representations or warranties, express or implied, about the outcome or methods of use of this publication, and assume no liability for claims, losses, or damages arising from the use or misuse of this publication. All responsibilities for legal effects or consequences of any document prepared from, or action taken in reliance upon information contained in this publication are disclaimed. The reader should not rely on this author or this publisher for any professional advice. Users of this publication intending to use this publication for preparation of legal documents are advised to check specifically on the current, applicable laws in any jurisdiction in which they intend the documents to be effective. Make sure you are using the most recent edition.

Is This Legal Self-Help Guide for You?

The Peerless Legal mission is to empower individuals by giving them legal self-help tools. The Legal Self-Help Guide series was created as the embodiment of that mission. The goal of this Guide is to provide you with the information you need to understand your legal rights and responsibilities. In doing so, we hope you will be able to resolve your legal issues yourself or know enough to feel confident in your decision to hire a licensed attorney. This Guide provides a meaningful alternative to most of the books in law libraries. Our goal is for you to be able to understand this material.

You are not alone in choosing legal self-help. Everyone faces legal issues at some point in their life. While most of us have the capacity to understand our legal rights and responsibilities, finding good legal information can be daunting. As the costs associated with legal representation rise, more and more people are opting to take certain legal matters into their own hands.

In this Guide, Peerless Legal provides you with meaningful alternatives to costly legal representation for legal issues you can handle yourself. This Guide is a plain-English alternative to the legal jargon that fills most legal books.

This book is for you if:

- you want to handle your own legal issues,
- you are not sure whether the legal issues you are facing merit the high cost of an attorney,
- you are in the process of looking for competent, legal representation, but are unsure how to evaluate legal services,
- you have retained an attorney and are unsure whether your attorney is competently handling your legal issues,
- or you want to know more about a specific legal topic.

It is important to manage expectations when acting on your own behalf or with an attorney. The forms in this book may differ from the forms that are commonly used in your local jurisdiction. You can check local rules by going to the court's website, by making a phone call to the office of the clerk of court, or by visiting a local law library. Generally, law school libraries serve as Federal repositories and are open to the public during normal business hours.

WARNING There are some legal issues that seem simple and straight forward, but in reality, only an attorney with extensive experience on the issue would know the inter-tangling.

Dedication

For my parents who taught me love and how to strive for the best, even when the best was difficult.

Acknowledgments

This book has been nothing short of a group effort. In addition to the above-named dedication, I would like to thank most my wife, who is also author of this book, for her gifts of motivation, support, and kind words.

About the Authors

Sanket Mistry earned his J.D. from Mercer Law School and is a member of the New York State Bar. He is a practicing lawyer and has published widely in landlord-tenant law and estate planning with over a dozen books in print and forthcoming. He has worked and volunteered at a number of government agencies, private organizations, and nonprofits. He also holds a B.A. in philosophy from Emory University and an M.I.A. from Columbia University. He is an avid painter and tennis player.

Nikita Mistry earned her Master's in law from NYU School of Law and an LL.B. from Amity Law School. She is a member of the New York State Bar and Bar Council of India. She is a practicing lawyer who has worked for several law firms in New York City as well as government agencies and nonprofits. She has served on the editorial boards of several law journals. She also holds a B.A. in political science from Amity Law School. She studies chess and is learning Spanish.

Please consider reviewing our book on <u>Amazon.com</u> or elsewhere.

Table of Contents

INTRODUCTION TO RENTING PROPERTY 1

OVERVIEW OF HOW TO RENT PROPERTY 2

I. INTRODUCTION TO RENTAL APPLICATIONS.. 3

1.   RENTAL APPLICATION CHECKLIST 4
2.   TENANT PRE-SCREENING QUESTIONS..5
3.   RECEIPT FOR PAYMENT 6
4.   RENTAL APPLICATION GUIDELINES 7
5.   RENTAL APPLICATION 10
6.   ESTIMATED MOVE-IN COSTS 16
7.   BROKERAGE DISCLOSURE 18
8.   AUTHORIZATION TO PERFORM CREDIT CHECKS AND CONTACT REFERENCES........... 19
9.   REQUEST FOR EMPLOYMENT REFERENCES 20
10. RENTAL HISTORY VERIFICATION 21
11. REQUEST FOR PERSONAL REFERENCES 22
12. WORKSHEET FOR PERSONAL REFERENCES RESPONSES 23
13. PAMPHLET 26
14. EMERGENCY CONTACTS 27
15. LOCAL SCHOOLS 28
16. TRANSPORTATION SERVICES 29
17. LOCAL GROCERY STORES 30
18. LOCAL RETAIL STORES 31
19. LOCAL ATTRACTIONS 32
20. ACCEPTANCE LETTER OF RENTAL APPLICATION 33
21. CONDITIONAL APPROVAL OF RENTAL APPLICATION... 34
22. DENIAL OF RENTAL APPLICATION 36

II. INTRODUCTION TO LEASE AGREEMENTS 38

23. LEASE AGREEMENT CHECKLIST.. 39
24. RECEIPT FOR PAYMENT 40
25. FIXED-TERM RESIDENTIAL LEASE AGREEMENT 41
26. MONTH-TO-MONTH RESIDENTIAL LEASE AGREEMENT 51
27. SELF-STORAGE ADDENDUM TO LEASE AGREEMENT 61
28. RENTER'S INSURANCE REQUIREMENTS 63
29. PET ADDENDUM TO LEASE AGREEMENT... 64
30. PARKING ADDENDUM TO LEASE AGREEMENT 65
31. VEHICLE REGISTRATION 67
32. KEY RELEASE ADDENDUM TO LEASE AGREEMENT 68
33. PROHIBITION AGAINST SHORT-TERM SUBLETTING OR RENTING ADDENDUM TO LEASE AGREEMENT...... 69
34. PACKAGE PICK-UP ADDENDUM TO LEASE AGREEMENT 71
35. SMOKE DETECTOR ADDENDUM TO LEASE AGREEMENT 72
36. CARBON MONOXIDE DETECTOR ADDENDUM TO LEASE AGREEMENT 73
37. ASBESTOS NOTIFICATION ADDENDUM TO LEASE AGREEMENT 74

38. PROPOSITION 65 ADDENDUM TO LEASE AGREEMENT (CALIFORNIA) 76
39. DISCLOSURE OF INFORMATION ON LEAD-BASED PAINT AND/OR LEAD-BASED PAINT HAZARDS 78
40. PROTECT YOUR FAMILY FROM LEAD IN YOUR HOME PAMPHLET 79
41. DECLARACIÓN DE INFORMACIÓN SOBRE PINTURA A BASE DE PLOMO Y/O PELIGROS DE LA PINTURA A BASE DE PLOMO 89
42. PROTEJA A SU FAMILIA CONTRA EL PLOMO EN EL HOGAR 90
43. MOLD PREVENTION AND CONTROL ADDENDUM TO LEASE AGREEMENT 100
44. PEST CONTROL DISCLOSURE NOTICE ADDENDUM TO LEASE AGREEMENT 103
45. BED BUG ADDENDUM TO LEASE AGREEMENT 106
46. SATELLITE, TELEVISION, AND INTERNET DISH/ANTENNA INSTALLATION POLICY AND RULES ADDENDUM TO LEASE AGREEMENT 110
47. CONSTRUCTION ADDENDUM TO LEASE AGREEMENT 114

III. INTRODUCTION TO MOVE-IN FORMS 115

48. MOVE-IN CHECKLIST 116
49. WELCOME LETTER 117
50. MOVE-IN WALK-THROUGH STATEMENT OF CONDITION 118
51. MOVE-IN WALK-THROUGH STATEMENT OF CONDITION SUPPLEMENT FOR FURNISHED PREMISES ... 122
52. UTILITIES CONTACT INFORMATION 127
53. PARKING POLICY 128
54. REFERRAL CARD 130
55. REPAIR REQUEST FORM 131

IV. INTRODUCTION TO LANDLORD FORMS 132

56. RECEIPT OF MONTHLY RENTAL PAYMENT 133
57. MONTHLY RENT PAYMENT RECORD LOG 134
58. INCREASE IN MONTHLY TENANT RENT LETTER 135
59. LANDLORD OFFER TO EXTEND LEASE AGREEMENT 136
60. ADDENDUM TO EXTEND LEASE AGREEMENT 137
61. ACCEPTANCE OF NOTICE OF INTENT TO VACATE 138
62. ADVANCED NOTICE TO ENTER PREMISES 140
63. PROOF OF SERVICE 141
64. NOTICE OF ENTRY OF RESIDENCE 142
65. NOTICE OF VIOLATION 144
66. CASH FOR KEYS AGREEMENT 145
67. RENTAL TERMINATION NOTICE 147
68. NOTICE TO VACATE 149
69. DEMAND TO MAKE GOOD ON BAD CHECK 151
70. AGREEMENT FOR DELAYED RENT PAYMENT 152
71. AGREEMENT FOR PARTIAL RENT PAYMENT 153
72. LATE RENT NOTICE 155
73. FINAL NOTICE OF FAILURE TO PAY RENT PRIOR TO LEGAL ACTION 156
74. NOTICE TO PAY RENT OR QUIT 157
75. CERTIFICATE OF SERVICE 158

V. INTRODUCTION TO MOVE-OUT FORMS 159

76. MOVE-OUT CHECKLIST 160

77.	MOVE-OUT LETTER	161
78.	MOVE-OUT CHECKLIST	163
79.	MOVE-OUT WALK-THROUGH STATEMENT OF CONDITION	164
80.	MOVE-OUT WALK-THROUGH STATEMENT OF CONDITION SUPPLEMENT FOR FURNISHED PREMISES	168
81.	MOVE-OUT INSPECTION LETTER	173
82.	LETTER OF SECURITY DEPOSIT RETURN	174
83.	ITEMIZED SECURITY DEPOSIT DEDUCTIONS	175

VI. INTRODUCTION TO TENANT FORMS 176

84.	APARTMENT HUNTING WORKSHEET	177
85.	REQUEST FOR CREDIT REPORT	178
86.	ROOMMATE AGREEMENT	179
87.	REQUEST TO ADD TENANT TO LEASE AGREEMENT	182
88.	REQUEST TO ASSIGN LEASE AGREEMENT	183
89.	ASSIGNMENT OF LEASE AGREEMENT	184
90.	TENANT REQUEST TO SUBLEASE	186
91.	SUBLEASE AGREEMENT	187
92.	HOUSE SITTING AGREEMENT	189
93.	TENANT REQUEST TO EXTEND LEASE AGREEMENT	192
94.	REPAIR REQUEST	193
95.	FOLLOW-UP REPAIR REQUEST	194
96.	NOTICE OF INSURANCE CLAIM FILED	195
97.	COMPLIANT LETTER TO LANDLORD	196
98.	NOTICE TO VACATE	197
99.	DEMAND LETTER FOR SECURITY DEPOSIT	198
100.	SECOND DEMAND LETTER FOR SECURITY DEPOSIT	199
101.	TENANT DISPUTE OF SECURITY DEPOSIT ITEMIZATION	200

VII. YOU CREATED YOUR LEGAL DOCUMENTS, NOW WHAT? 201

A.	Storing Documents	201
B.	Making Changes to Existing Documents	202

VIII. ADDITIONAL RESOURCES 204

A.	Attorneys	204
B.	Legal Research	205

Introduction to Renting Property

This book will help you in renting out your property, e.g. apartment, condo, spare room, converted basement. It will also help you to think about the legal documents as well as the real-life hurdles you may face as you go through your property rental journey. Getting your legal documents in order so that you can successfully create your own documents is key for landlords as well as tenants. For landlords, this book can prepare you for success with a potential passive income stream. With these documents, a landlord can gain a better understanding of the legal process to rent property. For Tenants, this book offers forms to help deal with issues tenants face as well as ideas on how to deal with common issues.

This book includes forms from the rental application to lease agreement to various addendums. It also includes some forms to help both the landlord and tenant deal with their unique situations. In addition, the book includes some basics of making these forms legal. It is worth noting that this book is not intended to be read as a novel. It is intended to be used as a reference guide. Pay attention to headings as well as the names of the forms because they are your guide-posts. This book is laid out in way to help you find information and forms quickly.

This book is written in plain-English with as little legal jargon as possible. However, sometimes the legal jargon cannot be avoided. This book is designed so that you can find information and forms on your legal topic quickly.

By the time you finish reading this book, you should be able to:
• successfully understand how to, and create, your own legal documents,
• know enough about your issue to determine whether it's complicated
• know enough to warrant hiring an attorney, and
• understand your legal rights and responsibilities.

The book begins with this basic legal information on how to make your documents legal. The information is a broad overview of the process. Not every piece of information will pertain to you or to your jurisdiction. More information about your jurisdiction is available online at the web addresses provided in the back of this book.

There is an introduction section at the beginning of each of the major topics. Think of these as previews of what is to come. Then there are check-lists intended to help you organize all of the various documents as well as serve as reminders to give to tenants. The check-lists can also be given to the tenants for their organization and reference as well. The remainder of the book is devoted to state information which provides links to information on each of the 50 states and the District of Columbia. Laws in different states vary and you should review this section to find your specific State rules.

The tools in this book will provide you with the information you need to create your documents or to equip you with the information you need to hire a competent attorney.

Overview of How to Rent Property

The first step to rent property is having a property. This book is not about finding rental property.

However, once you have the property to rent, then you can use this book. Below is a diagram to help you navigate the process. You will begin by understanding some of the basics of renting property e.g., knowing the local market and laws, what is the competition offering, what you are offering, and what is allowed and not allowed by law. Most of these come from experience in renting property and time. Once you have some basic knowledge, then you have to prepare the property for viewing by potential tenants, identify the terms you are willing to accept from a tenant, and identify a tenant – these steps run together. The aim is to find a potential tenant who can successfully complete a rental application and then a lease agreement. Some people will come see your place and decide they want different terms (e.g., a lower rent) so you will then start over by preparing the property. To help, this book includes some literature to give to potential tenants to help remember your property on their search.

After you find potential tenants, then they will complete a rental application. The potential tenants should sign the rental application and return it to you. A notary or observing signature is not required. Once the rental application has been completed, then you will need to do some due diligence such as checking credit scores, references, and verifying incomes. These are industry best practices, and you are generally free to be less or more selective, within lawful limits. You will then make a determination.

Next, once a successful rental application has been completed, a lease agreement and addendums will need to be completed. Again, a notary, witness, or observation of signatures is not required. Once all the signatures have been collected and money has been exchanged, the property has been leased and you can transfer over the keys. Now, you will manage the property until it is time for the tenants to move-out. The forms in this book can help you along the way.

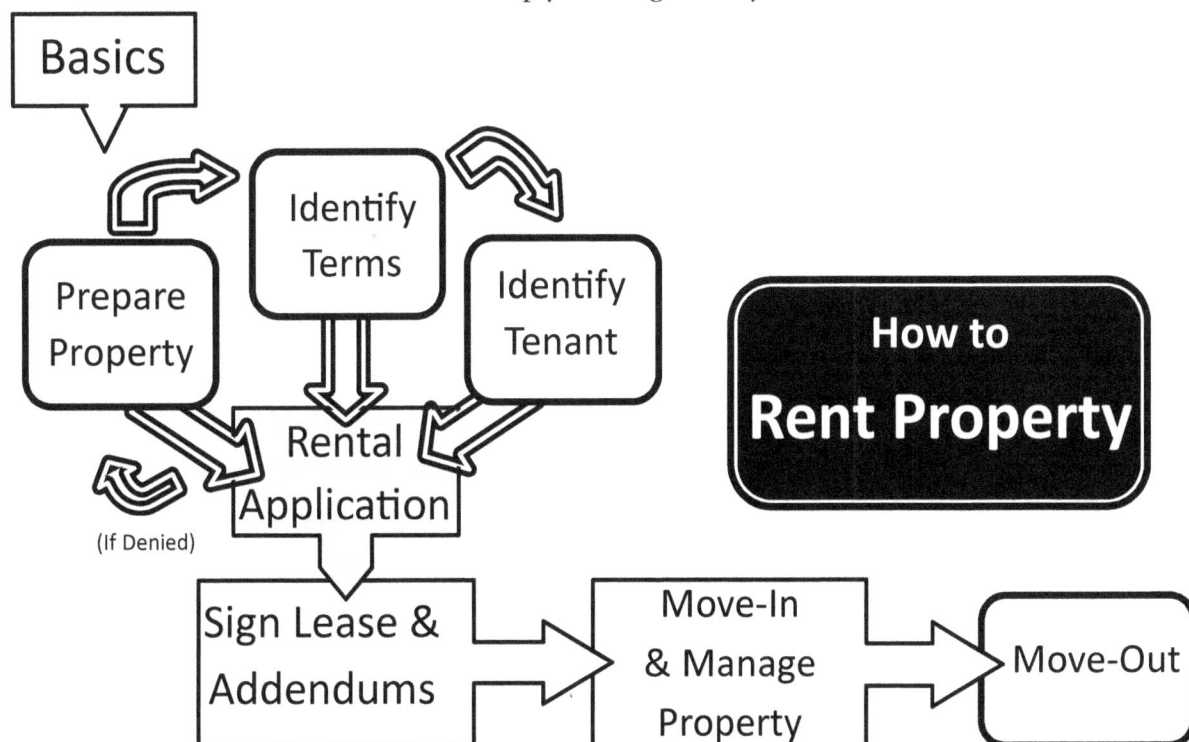

I.   Introduction to Rental Applications

Before you can rent property, you need to find a tenant. But you cannot just find just any tenant without knowing their financial reliability. Ideally, you want a tenant that pays their rent on time, doesn't cause damage to the property, and vacates the property once the lease ends. To help you find the ideal tenant, you have a few tools in which you may rely. This section provides some of those tools. After you have identified a potential tenant, you can use this section to help inform the potential tenant of the terms you are willing to accept, including:

- application fees,

- mandatory income verification methods,

- credit checks,

- minimum credit scores,

- pet and parking policies,

- rent payment schedules, and more.

The rental application is used to gather information on an applicant (a potential tenant) and help you make a reasonable determination as to whether you should rent to the applicant. The information that you collect should be for the purpose of determining the likelihood of the applicant being an ideal tenant. The rental application and applicant background check provide critical information about the applicant's background and history. By looking at income and other financial conditions, you can better gauge whether the applicant will be able to pay rent each month and/or cause damage to the property. There are no guarantees, but there are tools available to help make an informed decision.

Note that Federal, State, and local laws take discrimination very, very seriously and denying an applicant based on protected classes (e.g., race, gender, age, etc.) is strictly prohibited. As you review rental applications, it's important to understand and comply with all applicable fair housing laws. These laws prevent discrimination due to race, religion, ethnic background or nationality, gender, age, family status, disability and more. Credit checks from reputable companies and verifying employment history can help determine the reliability of various applicants while helping to avoid issues with fair housing laws (and others). Information that you collect should tell the financial picture of the applicant.

Rental Application Checklist

- ❑ Tenant Pre-Screening Questions
- ❑ Rental Application Guidelines
- ❑ Rental Application
- ❑ Estimated Move-In Costs
- ❑ Brokerage Disclosure
- ❑ Authorization to Perform Credit Check and Consent to Contact References
- ❑ Request for Employment References
- ❑ Rental History Verification
- ❑ Request for Personal Reference
- ❑ Pamphlet
- ❑ List of:

  - ❑ Emergency Contacts
  - ❑ Schools
  - ❑ Transportation Services
  - ❑ Grocery Stores
  - ❑ Retail Stores
  - ❑ Local Attractions

- ❑ _____
- ❑ _____
- ❑ _____
- ❑ _____

Comments: _____

_____

_____

_____

_____

_____

_____

_____

_____

_____

_____

_____

_____

_____

_____

Tenant Pre-Screening Questions

Date: _____   Landlord: _____

Phone: _____   E-mail: _____

      Address: _____

             _____

Tenant-Applicant: _____ Phone: _____ E-mail: _____

     Applicant: _____ Phone: _____ E-mail: _____

Completed Rental Application Includes:

$_____ Fee (Non-Refundable) ❑ Application Background Check ❑ Credit ❑ Income ❑ References

Pre-Screening Questions:

❑ How did you find this listing? _____

❑ Why are you moving? _____

❑ When do you plan on moving in? _____

❑ How many individuals will be living in the Premises? _____

❑ Will any pets be staying in the Premises? _____

❑ What is the household monthly income (before taxes)? _____

❑ Will you have a vehicle? ❑ No. ❑ Not sure. ❑ Yes. Number of vehicles? _____

❑ Do you plan on submitting a rental application? ❑ No. ❑ Undecided. ❑ Yes. _____

_____

Do you have any questions? _____

_____

Comments: _____

_____

_____

Receipt for Payment

Date Received: _____ Total Received $ _____

❑ Check ❑ Money Order Check No: _____ ❑ _____

Received from: _____

Premises Address: _____

_____

_____

Received by Landlord: _____

Address: _____

_____

_____

    Authorized signature: _____

Notes: _____

_____

_____

_____

_____

_____

_____

_____

_____

_____

_____

_____

_____

_____

_____

_____

_____

Rental Application Guidelines

Date: _____   Landlord: _____

Phone: _____   E-mail: _____

Address: _____

_____

Thank you for choosing your home with us. In order to process your Rental Application efficiently, please review this Rental Application Guidelines. Please note that you will have <u>72 hours</u> to submit all of the necessary paperwork or your application may be canceled.

Application Process

The following are required to process the application:
1) Completed Application;
2) Two original United States government issued forms of identification that meet the following requirements: one form of photo identification issued by the United States government (e.g., State-issued Driver's license or United States Passport), and a second form of identification issued by the United States government (e.g., Social Security Card, State-issued Driver's license, or United States Passport);
3) Fee; and
4) Proof of income.

Application Fee

All applicants must be 18 years of age or older. A $ _____ non-refundable application fee is required **per** applicant. The entire Rental Application must be completed before it will be accepted for processing. The application fee must be paid by money order, cashier's check, personal check, or other certified funds; cash will not be accepted.

Pick-Up and Go Fee

A Pick-Up and Go Administration Fee of $_____ at the time of application is required. This Fee will be returned if the application is rejected and forfeited in full if the applicant cancels forty-eight (48) hours after submitting the Rental Application.

Income Verification

A combined annual income of thirty-six (36) times the monthly rent is required. If the applicant does not have an annual income, he/she must have liquid assets equal to, or greater than, two hundred (200) times the monthly rent. A combination of annual salary and liquid assets may be taken into consideration.

If child support is calculated as part of the salary, a copy of court documents is required as proof of income.

A guarantor will be considered if the applicant has met all application qualifications standards with the exception of income or asset criteria. The guarantor must complete an application, meet all application qualification standards and provide proof of sixty (60) times the monthly rent in annual income or liquid assets in excess of four hundred (400) times the monthly rent. Guarantor must sign and have the guaranty form notarized. The original guarantor forms must be received prior to signing a lease.

7

Credit Worthiness

To determine your credit worthiness, the applicant's credit report, tenant history, references, and application data will be considered. An unacceptable credit reporting score for an applicant will necessitate an approved guarantor for a lease.

Deposit

A deposit, if any, will depend on the credit worthiness of the applicant. The deposit starts at the equivalent of one month's rent, but may be higher based on the application information. The deposits must be paid by money order, cashier's check, personal check, or other certified funds. Cash will not be accepted.

Utilities

Residents are responsible for all monthly utility payments **EXCEPT**: ❑ gas, ❑ electricity, ❑ water,

❑ sewer, ❑ trash, ❑ heat, ❑ hot water, ❑ Internet/WiFi, ❑ _____,

❑ _____, ❑ and_____.

Pets

❑ Pets are NOT allowed on the rental premises for long-term or short-term stays.

❑ Pets are allowed. No more than _____ pets in total are allowed per rental premises. A signed pet addendum is required prior to pet move-in.

> ❑ All dogs require liability insurance coverage prior to being brought onto the premises. Dogs have an upfront fee of $_____ which ❑ is/❑ is not refundable. An ongoing monthly pet rental fee of $_____ per dog. The combined weight limit of all of the dogs in the Premises is _____ pounds. Please check for breed restrictions.

> ❑ Cats have an upfront fee of $_____ which ❑ is/❑ is not refundable and an ongoing monthly pet rental fee of $_____ per cat.

❑ Other animals (e.g., fish, birds, hamsters) require prior approval and fees.

Large aquariums are not permitted on the rental premises.

Parking

❑ Parking is NOT provided. ❑ Street parking is available.

❑ Free parking is provided for _____ number of vehicles. ❑ Additional vehicles will be provided for a monthly fee of $_____. The license plate number, make, and model of all vehicles will be required to be disclosed to the landlord as well as all vehicles on the rental premises. Also, a copy of the applicant's State-issued driver's license is required. ❑ Street parking is available.

❑ Parking is provided for a monthly fee of $_____. The license plate number, make, and model of all vehicles will be required to be disclosed to the landlord as well as all vehicles on the rental premises. Also, a copy of the applicant's State-issued driver's license is required. ❑ Street parking is available.

First Month's Rent

The first month's rent must be paid in full at the time of lease signing. If your move-in date occurs <u>on or after</u> the 25th of any month, you will be required to pay the pro-rated rent for the remainder of the month plus the rent for the following month at the time of lease signing.

Occupancy

Occupancy is restricted to two (2) people per bedroom, plus one (1) additional person e.g., two (2) people may reside in a studio or efficiency Premises, three (3) people in a one (1) bedroom Premises.

Renter's Insurance

All applicants must maintain renter's insurance starting on the first day of the lease. Proof of renter's insurance will be required at lease signing. **Minimum requirements are as follows: $_____ personal liability and $_____personal property coverage.** Applicants may choose an insurance provider of their choice.

Prior Residences

If you state that you have never lived anywhere other than at home or with relatives, no other address should appear on your credit report. If you are renting a private residence, you must present the last three cancelled checks or money order receipts that show payment of rent. Any misrepresentation on your rental application may result in a denial.

Foreign Nationals

Income must be earned in United States dollars and deposited into United States financial institutions. A guarantor located in the United States is required, if the applicant is unable to provide income verification within the United States. For international students, an I-20 Visa will be accepted as a form of income and the same combined annual income of thirty-six (36) times the monthly rent is required.

Waterbeds

Waterbeds are prohibited on the rental premises.

Prohibition Against Short-Term Subletting or Renting

Renting out of the Premises through short-term subletting or renting (e.g., Airbnb, or its equivalent), is **NOT** permitted. Any violations will be cause for termination of the lease and possible loss of deposit. Also, any violations of city, county, state, and/or Federal ordinances or other regulations related to restrictions on short-term rentals will be forwarded to the proper authorities.

Smoking

Smoking in the Premises is ❑ strictly prohibited ❑ allowed.

Rental Application

This application is hereby made to rent the "Premises" located at: _____

_____

_____

under a lease of _____ months beginning on the _____ day of _____, 20_____
at a monthly rental of $_____ payable in advance on the first of each month.

Utilities included in monthly rent: ❑ Gas   ❑ Electricity   ❑ Water   ❑ Sewer

     ❑ Trash   ❑ Heat   ❑ Hot Water   ❑Internet/WiFi ❑ _____

     ❑ _____   ❑ _____

     ❑ _____   ❑ _____

The remaining utilities are not included as part of the monthly rent.

There ❑ is/ ❑ is NOT a petition for rent adjustment currently pending for the Premises. If a petition for a rent adjustment is currently pending, the petition number is _____, which is dated _____.

In consideration of a lease agreement, the undersigned Applicant hereby submits the following information concerning the occupant(s) of the Premises for which this application is made. It is understood that the Premises is to be used only as a residence to be occupied at maximum by two (2) people per bedroom, plus one (1) additional person e.g., two (2) people may reside in a studio or efficiency Premises, three (3) people in a one (1) bedroom Premises. Under normal occupancy, no more than ___ persons may occupy the Premises. **The property is accepted "AS IS" unless otherwise noted below or by an addendum.**

APPLICANT'S NAME: _____ SSN: _____

     Date of Birth: _____ Driver's License No./State: _____

     Telephone: _____ Telephone: _____

     Email Address: _____

PRESENT ADDRESS: _____

     Dates From: _____ To: _____

     Present Landlord/Mortgage Co.: _____

     Monthly Payment $_____. Reason for moving: _____

PREVIOUS ADDRESS: _____

    Dates From: _____ To: _____

    Present Landlord/Mortgage Co.: _____

    Monthly Payment $_____. Reason for moving: _____

SOURCE OF INCOME/EMPLOYER: _____ Gross Monthly Income $ _____

    Title/Occupation: _____ Starting Date: _____

    Contact Name: _____ Telephone: _____

    Contact Address: _____

ADDITIONAL APPLICANT'S NAME: _____ SSN: _____

    Date of Birth: _____ Driver's License No./State: _____

    Telephone: _____ Telephone: _____

    Email Address: _____

PRESENT ADDRESS: _____

    Dates From: _____ To: _____

    Present Landlord/Mortgage Co.: _____

    Monthly Payment $_____. Reason for moving: _____

PREVIOUS ADDRESS: _____

    Dates From: _____ To: _____

    Present Landlord/Mortgage Co.: _____

    Monthly Payment $_____. Reason for moving: _____

SOURCE OF INCOME/EMPLOYER: _____ Gross Monthly Income $ _____

    Title/Occupation: _____ Starting Date: _____

    Contact Name: _____ Telephone: _____

    Contact Address: _____

ADDITIONAL APPLICANT'S NAME: _____ SSN: _____

    Date of Birth: _____ Driver's License No./State: _____

    Telephone: _____ Telephone: _____

    Email Address: _____

PRESENT ADDRESS: _____

    Dates From: _____ To: _____

    Present Landlord/Mortgage Co.: _____

    Monthly Payment $_____. Reason for moving: _____

PREVIOUS ADDRESS: _____

    Dates From: _____ To: _____

    Present Landlord/Mortgage Co.: _____

    Monthly Payment $_____. Reason for moving: _____

SOURCE OF INCOME/EMPLOYER: _____ Gross Monthly Income $ _____

    Title/Occupation: _____ Starting Date: _____

    Contact Name: _____ Telephone: _____

    Contact Address: _____

ADDITIONAL APPLICANT'S NAME: _____ SSN: _____

    Date of Birth: _____ Driver's License No./State: _____

    Telephone: _____ Telephone: _____

    Email Address: _____

PRESENT ADDRESS: _____

    Dates From: _____ To: _____

    Present Landlord/Mortgage Co.: _____

    Monthly Payment $_____. Reason for moving: _____

PREVIOUS ADDRESS: _____

    Dates From: _____ To: _____

    Present Landlord/Mortgage Co.: _____

    Monthly Payment $_____. Reason for moving: _____

SOURCE OF INCOME/EMPLOYER: _____ Gross Monthly Income $ _____

    Title/Occupation: _____ Starting Date: _____

    Contact Name: _____ Telephone: _____

    Contact Address: _____

EMERGENCY CONTACTS (Relatives or persons not living with Applicant(s))

    Name: _____ Relationship: _____

    Telephone: _____ Telephone: _____

    Contact Address: _____

    Name: _____ Relationship: _____

    Telephone: _____ Telephone: _____

    Contact Address: _____

A non-refundable application fee of $ _____, and a non-refundable administrative/pick-up and go cleaning fee of $ _____ is required to complete this Application to rent to cover the costs associated with obtaining a credit report and processing this Application. A deposit of $ _____ against the first month's rent is also required. The application fee is non-refundable. **The deposit and administrative/pick-up and go cleaning fee will be refunded only if Applicant is not approved or if Applicant cancels within 48 hours after the date of this Application. If Applicant is approved but fails to execute a lease, the deposit will be forfeited as liquidation damages to Owner in consideration of its having reserved the Premises for Applicant.** Applicant specifically understands and agrees, however, that acceptance of fees and the deposit in no way obligates the Owner to offer a lease to Applicant, and Applicant's right to a lease is expressly contingent on the Owner's acceptance and approval of this Application.

Applicant hereby acknowledges receipt of an exact, legible, and complete copy of this executed Rental Application.

APPLICANT SIGNATURE: _____ DATE: _____

APPLICANT SIGNATURE: _____ DATE: _____

APPLICANT SIGNATURE: _____ DATE: _____

APPLICANT SIGNATURE: _____ DATE: _____

Fees and deposit paid in full acknowledged on behalf of Owner Landlord by:

_____ DATE: _____

It is unlawful to discriminate on the basis of race, color, religion, national origin, sex, age, marital status, personal appearance, sexual orientation, familial status, family responsibilities, matriculation, political affiliation, disability, source of income, or place of residence or business. This Rental Application will be processed in accordance with all Fair Housing and occupancy laws.

On notice to Applicant of Owner's acceptance and approval of the Rental Application, Applicant agrees to immediately execute a lease agreement for the Premises and to pay any balance due for the first month's rent, deposits, plus the Pick-Up and Go Fee, along with any other fees related to taking possession of the Premises. In the event the Applicant fails to execute a lease agreement and pay said fees within five (5) calendar days after notification of Owner's acceptance and approval of this application, the Applicant will automatically be deemed to be withdrawn from the Application and the Owner will be free to rent the Premises to another party without liability to Applicant, and the Pick-Up and Go Fee will be forfeited as liquidation damages to defray lost rents, expenses, and other damages resulting from Applicant's failure to lease the Premises. In the event the application is not accepted, the Pick-Up and Go Fee will be refunded to Applicant.

Nothing contained in this Application will be deemed to create liability on the part of the Owner for failure to deliver the Premises on the beginning date specified above, or will anything in this Application be deemed to release the Applicant from any liability created by this Application to lease the Premises, except, in the event of a delay in the delivery of possession, the monthly rent stipulated will be abated on a pro-rated basis until such time as the Applicant could have taken possession of the Premises. If, however, Owner is unable to deliver possession of the Premises to Applicant within thirty (30) calendar days of the proposed move-in date, either party may terminate this application and/or the lease agreement on written notice to the other party given prior to the delivery of possession.

In order to induce the Owner to offer a lease agreement to the Applicant, Applicant authorizes the Owner to verify any and all of the information contained in this Application, and Applicant releases all persons involved in the verification of such information from any and all liability arising therefrom. Applicant acknowledges that the Owner or its agent will obtain an investigative consumer credit report(s), credit and personal references, and to perform criminal background investigations on all persons to occupy the

Premises. In accordance with the fair credit reporting act (15 U.S.C. Section 1681D(B)), Applicant is hereby advised that he/she has the right to make a written request within a reasonable time for a complete and accurate disclosure of the nature and scope of the investigation conducted in connection with this application.

Applicant agrees and affirms that all of the information and all of the questions on this application have been fully and honestly answered; that the answers set forth in this application are complete, true, and correct; and that Applicant has not failed to disclose any information which, if disclosed, might tend to cause the Owner to consider this application less favorably. Applicant agrees that in the event any information or representation contained in this application is found to be inaccurate, Owner has the right to deny the application or to terminate any lease agreement entered into with the Applicant based on the information contained in this application.

Estimated Move-In Costs

Date: _____   Estimated Move-In Date: _____

Address: _____

_____

Applicant Name(s): _____

_____

Lease Term: ❑ Fixed term of _____ Months   ❑ Month-to-Month

Description	Unit Price	Total Amount
Rent	$	$
Pro-Rated Rent	$	$
Security Deposit	$	$
*Other Deposit	$	$
App and Pick-Up and Go Fees	$	$
Pet Premium	$	$
Parking Premium	$	$
Other:	$	$
Other:	$	$
Other:	$	$
Other:	$	$
Total:		**$**
Received:		**Total Amount**
Move-In Concession		$
Fees		$
Other:		$
Other:		$
Total Due at Move-In:		**$**

Make payable to: _____

All fees must be paid by money order, cashier's check, personal checks, or other certified funds; no cash will be accepted.

---

*Pro-Rated Rent: A full month's rent is due at move-in. If moving in on the 25th day of the month or later, the pro-rated rent is also due at move-in. If moving in prior to the 25th day of the month, the pro-rated rent is due the following month.

*Deposits: are based on approved credit and is subject to change based on rental, employment, and credit history.

Utility Services: Residents are responsible for all monthly utility payments, except: ❑ gas, ❑ electricity, ❑ water, ❑ sewer, ❑ trash, ❑ heat, ❑ hot water, ❑ Internet/WiFi, ❑ _____ ❑ _____, and ❑ _____

Renter's Insurance: General Liability coverage of $_____ AND Personal Property coverage of $_____ is required prior to move-in.

Application Fees Are Non-Refundable.

Notes:_____

_____

_____

Application Authorization

I have read the above statements, understand this is an estimate and am in agreement.

APPLICANT SIGNATURE: _____ DATE: _____

APPLICANT SIGNATURE: _____ DATE: _____

APPLICANT SIGNATURE: _____ DATE: _____

APPLICANT SIGNATURE: _____ DATE: _____

Prepared By: _____

Address: _____

_____

Landlord/Authorized Signature: _____

Brokerage Disclosure

The Applicant acknowledges by initials that in this real estate leasing transaction, the Listing Broker,

_____

_____

_____,

represents ❑ the Landlord **OR** ❑ the Tenant. (If the Broker is acting as a dual representative of both the Landlord and Tenant, then the appropriate disclosure form is attached to and made a part of this Rental Application.

Applicant(s) Initials _____ / _____ / _____ / _____

Leasing Agent must attach a business card

Applicant(s) Identification Type and Expiration Date: _____

_____

_____

_____

Notes:_____

_____

_____

_____

_____

_____

_____

_____

_____

_____

_____

_____

Authorization to Perform Credit Checks and Contact References

Applicant Authorization

I authorize release of my credit sources (e.g., credit rating agencies), employers, current and previous landlords, and personal references, as part of a rental application. I give permission for the landlord or its agents to obtain a consumer report about me to ensure that I continue to meet the terms of the tenancy, for the collection and recovery of any financial obligations relating to my tenancy, and for any other reasonable permissible purpose.

Applicant Name: _____

Applicant Address: _____

_____

_____

Applicant Signature: _____ Date: _____

Landlord Signature: _____

Rental Address: _____

_____

_____

Applicant rights under the Fair Credit Reporting Act (FCRA) (15 U.S.C. §§ 1681 et seq) and the Fair and Accurate Credit Transactions (FACT) Act of 2003 (Pub.L. 108–159).

Request for Employment References

Applicant Authorization

      I authorize release of my employment information to provide employment references as part of a rental application.

Applicant Name: _____

Applicant Signature: _____ Date: _____

Employer: _____ Gross Monthly Income $ _____

Title/Occupation: _____ Starting Date: _____

Contact Name: _____ Phone: _____

Contact Address: _____

_____

The Applicant listed above has made a rental application. As part of their application, please take a moment to fill out this Reference. Thank you in advance for a prompt response.

Employer contact name, title, and relation to applicant:_____

_____

_____

1. Can you verify whether the Applicant's employment, job title, pay, and starting date listed above are correct? ❑ Yes ❑ No, please explain: _____

   _____

   _____

2. Is the Applicant currently employed there? ❑ Yes ❑ No, please explain: _____

   _____

   _____

3. How long has the Applicant worked there? _____

4. Are there any anticipated changes in their salary or employment status in the next year?

   ❑ No ❑ Yes, please explain: _____

   _____

   _____

Rental History Verification

Applicant Authorization

I authorize release of my rental history as part of a rental application .

Applicant Name: _____

Applicant Signature: _____ Date: _____

Previous Address: _____

_____

_____

Contact Name: _____ Phone: _____

The Applicant listed above has made a rental application. As part of their application, please take a moment to fill out this Verification. Thank you in advance for a prompt response.

1. Please verify the above address: ❑ Yes ❑ No, please explain: _____

_____

_____

2. What was the Applicant's move in date: _____

3. Did the Applicant pay on time? ❑ Yes ❑ No, please explain: _____

_____

4. Was the Applicant past due in paying rent? ❑ Yes ❑ No; If yes, number times in last year: _____

5. Have you ever had any problems with the Applicant? ❑ Yes ❑ No; If yes, please explain: _____

_____

6. Did you receive sufficient notice of Applicant's intent to move? ❑ Yes ❑ No

7. Would you re-rent to this Applicant? ❑ Yes ❑ No, please explain: _____

_____

8. Would you recommend this Applicant to a landlord? ❑ Yes ❑ No, please explain: _____

_____

_____

Comments: _____

_____

_____

Signature: _____ Title: _____ Date: _____

Request for Personal References

Applicant Authorization

    I authorize release of my information to provide personal references as part of a rental application.

Applicant Name: _____

Applicant Signature: _____ Date: _____

Reference #1:

Name: _____Relationship: _____

Occupation: _____ Phone: _____

Address: _____

_____

Reference #2:

Name: _____Relationship: _____

Occupation: _____ Phone: _____

Address: _____

_____

Reference #3:

Name: _____Relationship: _____

Occupation: _____ Phone: _____

Address: _____

_____

Worksheet for Personal References Responses

REFERENCE# 1 Name: _____   Phone: _____

The Applicant, _____, has made a rental application and have listed you as a personal reference. Please answer the following questions as honestly and fully as you can. Feel free to ask for clarification if needed.

---

1. Are you willing to provide a personal reference for the Applicant? ❑ Yes ❑ No, please explain:

    _____

    _____

2. What is your relationship to the Applicant? _____

3. How long have you known the Applicant? _____

4. Please describe the character of the Applicant: _____

    _____

    _____

5. Would you recommend this Applicant to a landlord? ❑ Yes ❑ No; If yes, please explain: _____

    _____

    _____

Comments: _____

_____

_____

_____

_____

_____

_____

_____

Worksheet for Personal References Responses

REFERENCE #2 Name: _____   Phone: _____

The Applicant, _____, has made a rental application and have listed you as a personal reference. Please answer the following questions as honestly and fully as you can. Feel free to ask for clarification if needed.

1. Are you willing to provide a personal reference for the Applicant? ❑ Yes ❑ No, please explain:

   _____

   _____

2. What is your relationship to the Applicant? _____

3. How long have you known the Applicant? _____

4. Please describe the character of the Applicant: _____

   _____

   _____

5. Would you recommend this Applicant to a landlord? ❑ Yes ❑ No; If yes, please explain: _____

   _____

   _____

Comments: _____

_____

_____

_____

_____

_____

_____

_____

_____

_____

Worksheet for Personal References Responses

REFERENCE# 3 Name: _____   Phone: _____

The Applicant, _____, has made a rental application and have listed you as a personal reference. Please answer the following questions as honestly and fully as you can. Feel free to ask for clarification if needed.

1. Are you willing to provide a personal reference for the Applicant? ❑ Yes ❑ No, please explain:

    _____

    _____

2. What is your relationship to the Applicant? _____

3. How long have you known the Applicant? _____

4. Please describe the character of the Applicant: _____

    _____

    _____

5. Would you recommend this Applicant to a landlord? ❑ Yes ❑ No; If yes, please explain: _____

    _____

    _____

Comments: _____

_____

_____

_____

_____

_____

_____

_____

_____

Pamphlet

Date: _____   Estimated Move-In Date: _____

Landlord Name: _____

Premises Address: _____

_____

_____

Phone: _____   Phone: _____

E-mail: _____   Website: _____

Lease Terms: _____ Months or   ❏ Month-to-Month

❏ Unfurnished   or   ❏ Furnished

Monthly Rent: $ _____   Security Deposit: $ _____

Application Fee: $ _____   Pick-Up and Go Fee: $ _____

Number of Bedrooms: ❏ Studio   ❏ 1 ❏ 2   ❏ 3   ❏ Note: _____

Number of Bathrooms: ❏ Half +   ❏ 1 ❏ 2   ❏ 3   ❏ Note: _____

Approximate: _____ Sq. Ft.

Notes: _____

_____

_____

Diagram of the property:

Emergency Contacts

Facility Manager: _____ Phone: _____

    Alternate Phone: _____

Utility Company: _____ Phone: _____

Utility Company: _____ Phone: _____

Utility Company: _____ Phone: _____

Animal Control: _____

    Address: _____

    Phone: _____ Website: _____

Police Station: _____

    Address: _____

    Phone: _____ Website: _____

Hospital: _____

    Address: _____

    Phone: _____ Website: _____

Fire Station: _____

    Address: _____

    Phone: _____ Website: _____

Other: _____

    Address: _____

    Phone: _____ Website: _____

Other: _____

    Address: _____

    Phone: _____ Website: _____

Local Schools

Elementary: _____

    Address: _____

    Phone: _____ Website: _____

Elementary: _____

    Address: _____

    Phone: _____ Website: _____

Middle School: _____

    Address: _____

    Phone: _____ Website: _____

Middle School: _____

    Address: _____

    Phone: _____ Website: _____

High School: _____

    Address: _____

    Phone: _____ Website: _____

High School: _____

    Address: _____

    Phone: _____ Website: _____

Other: _____

    Address: _____

    Phone: _____ Website: _____

Transportation Services

Nearby public transportation: _____

    Address: _____

    Phone: _____ Website: _____

Nearby public transportation: _____

    Address: _____

    Phone: _____ Website: _____

Nearby public transportation: _____

    Address: _____

    Phone: _____ Website: _____

Taxi: _____

    Address: _____

    Phone: _____ Website: _____

Taxi: _____

    Address: _____

    Phone: _____ Website: _____

Other: _____

    Address: _____

    Phone: _____ Website: _____

Other: _____

    Address: _____

    Phone: _____ Website: _____

Local Grocery Stores

Store: _____

    Address: _____

    Phone: _____ Website: _____

Store: _____

    Address: _____

    Phone: _____ Website: _____

Store: _____

    Address: _____

    Phone: _____ Website: _____

Store: _____

    Address: _____

    Phone: _____ Website: _____

Store: _____

    Address: _____

    Phone: _____ Website: _____

Store: _____

    Address: _____

    Phone: _____ Website: _____

Store: _____

    Address: _____

    Phone: _____ Website: _____

Local Retail Stores

Store: _____

    Address: _____

    Phone: _____ Website: _____

Store: _____

    Address: _____

    Phone: _____ Website: _____

Store: _____

    Address: _____

    Phone: _____ Website: _____

Store: _____

    Address: _____

    Phone: _____ Website: _____

Store: _____

    Address: _____

    Phone: _____ Website: _____

Store: _____

    Address: _____

    Phone: _____ Website: _____

Store: _____

    Address: _____

    Phone: _____ Website: _____

Store: _____

    Address: _____

    Phone: _____ Website: _____

Local Attractions

Place: _____

    Address: _____

    Phone: _____ Website: _____

Place: _____

    Address: _____

    Phone: _____ Website: _____

Place: _____

    Address: _____

    Phone: _____ Website: _____

Place: _____

    Address: _____

    Phone: _____ Website: _____

Place: _____

    Address: _____

    Phone: _____ Website: _____

Place: _____

    Address: _____

    Phone: _____ Website: _____

Place: _____

    Address: _____

    Phone: _____ Website: _____

Acceptance Letter of Rental Application

Applicant Address: _____

_____

_____

Date: _____

Dear: _____,

Congratulations! I am pleased to notify you that your rental application to rent the property at:

_____

has been approved. This Letter serves as a formal confirmation of your rental application's acceptance.

Your lease begins on _____ at: $_____/month.

Fees that have already been paid will go towards the lease agreement.

I want to thank you for your application, and I hope that you will have an enjoyable living experience in your new home.

If you have any questions or concerns, please feel free to contact me.

    Sincerely,

    Landlord Signature: _____

    Printed Name: _____

    Address: _____

    _____

    _____

    Phone: _____

    E-Mail: _____

Conditional Approval of Rental Application

Applicant Address: _____

_____

_____

Date: _____

Dear: _____,

Your rental application to rent the property located at: _____

_____

has been conditionally approved. The condition is on your ability and willingness to: _____

_____

_____

Applicant rights under the Fair Credit Reporting Act (FCRA) (15 U.S.C. §§ 1681 et seq) and the Fair and Accurate Credit Transactions (FACT) Act of 2003 (Pub.L. 108–159).

We have conditionally approved your application for the following reason(s):

❑ **Consumer Credit Report (see below).**

> ❑ Information in a consumer credit report obtained from the Consumer Credit Reporting Agency named below.

> ❑ A consumer credit report containing insufficient information obtained from the Consumer Credit Reporting Agency named below.

> *You have a right to know the information contained in your credit file at the Consumer Credit Reporting Agency. You also have a right to a free copy of your report from the Consumer Credit Reporting Agency, if you request it no later than 60 days after you receive this Notice or if you have not requested a free copy within the past year. In addition, if you find that any information contained in the report you receive is inaccurate or incomplete, you have the right to dispute the matter with the Consumer Credit Reporting Agency. The Consumer Credit Reporting Agency must reinvestigate within a reasonable amount of time, free of charge, and remove and/or change inaccurate information. If the reinvestigation does not resolve the dispute to your satisfaction, you have the right to add you own "Consumer Statement" within 100 words (depending on the Agency's policies) to your official consumer credit report that must be included in future reports (or a clear summary depending on the Agency's policies). For further information, you can contact your state or local consumer protection agency or your state's attorney general's office.*

❑ **Score from a Consumer Credit Reporting Agency.** Your credit score was obtained from the Consumer Credit Reporting Agency named below. Your credit score is a number that reflects the information in your credit report. Your credit score can change, depending on how the information in your credit report changes. Scores range from a low 300 to a high 850.

Your credit score: _____   Date Obtained: _____

If you have any questions regarding your credit score, you should contact the Consumer Credit Reporting Agency named below.

❑ **Guarantor not accepted.**

❑ **Co-Applicant not accepted.**

❑ **Information received from a person or company other than a Consumer Credit Reporting Agency.** You have a right to learn of the nature of the information, if you ask us in writing within 60 days of the date of this Notice.

The Consumer Credit Reporting Agency that provided the report and/or credit score (if applicable) that influenced our decision in whole or in part is listed below. The Consumer Credit Reporting Agency played no part in our decision, and is unable to supply specific reasons why we have conditionally approved your rental application:

Consumer Credit Reporting Agency Name: _____

    Address: _____

    _____

    _____

    Phone _____ Website: _____

Applicant rights under the Fair Credit Reporting Act (FCRA) (15 U.S.C. §§ 1681 et seq) and the Fair and Accurate Credit Transactions (FACT) Act of 2003 (Pub.L. 108–159). For further information, you can contact your state or locate consumer protection agency, or your state's attorney general's office.

Sincerely,

Landlord Signature: _____

Printed Name: _____

Address: _____

_____

_____

Phone: _____

E-Mail: _____

Denial of Rental Application

Applicant Address: _____

_____

_____

Date: _____

Dear: _____,

Applicant rights under the Fair Credit Reporting Act (FCRA) (15 U.S.C. §§ 1681 et seq) and the Fair and Accurate Credit Transactions (FACT) Act of 2003 (Pub.L. 108–159).

Your rental application to rent the property located at: _____

_____

has been denied for the following reasons:

❑ **Consumer Credit Report (see below).**

    ❑ Information in a consumer credit report obtained from the Consumer Credit Reporting Agency named below.

    ❑ A consumer credit report containing insufficient information obtained from the Consumer Credit Reporting Agency named below.

    You have a right to know the information contained in your credit file at the Consumer Credit Reporting Agency. You also have a right to a free copy of your report from the Consumer Credit Reporting Agency, if you request it no later than 60 days after you receive this Notice or if you have not requested a free copy within the past year. In addition, if you find that any information contained in the report you receive is inaccurate or incomplete, you have the right to dispute the matter with the Consumer Credit Reporting Agency. The Consumer Credit Reporting Agency must reinvestigate within a reasonable amount of time, free of charge, and remove and/or change inaccurate information. If the reinvestigation does not resolve the dispute to your satisfaction, you have the right to add you own "Consumer Statement" within 100 words (depending on the Agency's policies) to your official consumer credit report that must be included in future reports (or a clear summary depending on the Agency's policies). For further information, you can contact your state or local consumer protection agency or your state's attorney general's office.

❑ **Score from a Consumer Credit Reporting Agency.** Your credit score was obtained from the Consumer Credit Reporting Agency named below. Your credit score is a number that reflects the information in your credit report. Your credit score can change, depending on how the information in your credit report changes. Scores range from a low 300 to a high 850.

Your credit score: _____   Date Obtained: _____

If you have any questions regarding your credit score, you should contact the Consumer Credit Reporting Agency named below.

❑ **Guarantor not accepted.**

❑ **Co-Applicant not accepted.**

❑ **Information received from a person or company other than a Consumer Credit Reporting Agency.** You have a right to learn of the nature of the information, if you ask us in writing within 60 days of the date of this Notice.

The Consumer Credit Reporting Agency that provided the report and/or credit score (if applicable) that influenced our decision in whole or in part is listed below. The Consumer Credit Reporting Agency played no part in our decision, and is unable to supply specific reasons why we have conditionally approved your rental application:

Consumer Credit Reporting Agency Name: _____

Address: _____

_____

_____

Phone _____ Website: _____

Applicant rights under the Fair Credit Reporting Act (FCRA) (15 U.S.C. §§ 1681 et seq) and the Fair and Accurate Credit Transactions (FACT) Act of 2003 (Pub.L. 108–159). For further information, you can contact your state or locate consumer protection agency, or your state's attorney general's office.

Enclosed are the deposit, if any, and fee refunds. Total amount enclosed is $ _____.

Sincerely,

Landlord Signature: _____

Printed Name: _____

Address: _____

_____

_____

Phone: _____

E-Mail: _____

II.   Introduction to Lease Agreements

A lease agreement is a legal contract that outlines each party's rights and obligations. As a landlord, you want a tenant to pay rent on time and take care of the property. You also want the tenant to vacate the property timely and without leaving a mess. A lease agreement is a tool that helps both parties follow through on their end of the bargain. In addition to the exchange of money, a lease agreement requires the exchange of promises (or covenants) as well as dealing in good faith (i.e., lie or deceive the other party for example by fabricating damages to retain a security deposit).

The more transparent and clear a lease agreement, the more likely it is to be read and followed. After all, you want important rules and information to be read and understood by your tenant before a tenant enters into the lease agreement.

Lease agreements help protect both parties by providing information upfront and by reducing the likelihood of legal headaches down the road. When both parties review and sign the lease agreement, there should be no confusion about what is expected from either party. Both parties should ask the other questions about the lease agreement to help clarity. The lease agreements provided stipulate that all prior oral agreements are merged into the lease agreement so what is in the lease agreement will likely be controlling. So, if you prefer other language, then make the adjustments accordingly in writing. If you end up in a legal battle, the written lease agreement may be looked at by the courts.

A lease agreement may help you in court, so you should keep detailed records of the:

- lease agreement,

- any exchange of money, including monthly rent,

- addendums (e.g., self-storage, pets, parking, vehicle registration, detectors, mold)

- security deposits,

- move-in checklists,

- written notices (e.g., notice of entry, late rent, rent increase),

- records of repair requests and receipts for repairs, and

- all correspondences with the tenant.

This section provides many of the forms that you should keep.

Lease Agreement Checklist

Date: _____   Landlord: _____

Phone: _____   E-mail: _____

    Address: _____

    _____

Renter: _____ Phone: _____ E-mail: _____

Copies Provided:

- ❑ Lease Agreement Checklist
- ❑ Lease Agreement
- ❑ Self-Storage Addendum to Lease Agreement
- ❑ Renter's Insurance Requirements
- ❑ Pet Addendum to Lease Agreement
- ❑ Parking Addendum to Lease Agreement
- ❑ Vehicle Registration
- ❑ Key Release Addendum to Lease Agreement
- ❑ Prohibition Against Short-Term Subletting or Renting Addendum to Lease Agreement
- ❑ Package Pick-up Addendum to Lease Agreement
- ❑ Smoke Detector Addendum to Lease Agreement
- ❑ Carbon Monoxide Detector Addendum to Lease Agreement
- ❑ Asbestos Notification Addendum to Lease Agreement
- ❑ Proposition 65 Addendum to Lease Agreement (California)
- ❑ Disclosure of Information on Lead-Based Paint and Lead-Based Paint Hazards Addendum to Lease Agreement
- ❑ EPA Lead-Based Paint Pamphlet
- ❑ Mold Prevention and Control Addendum to Lease Agreement
- ❑ Pest Control Disclosure Notice Addendum to Lease Agreement
- ❑ Bed bug Addendum to Lease Agreement
- ❑ Satellite, Television, and Internet Dish/Antenna Installation Policy and Rules Addendum to Agreement
- ❑ Construction Addendum to Lease Agreement
- ❑ _____
- ❑ _____
- ❑ _____
- ❑ _____

Comments: _____

_____

_____

Receipt for Payment

Date Received: _____ Total Received $ _____

❑ Check ❑ Money Order Check No: _____ ❑ _____

Received from: _____

Premises Address: _____

_____

_____

Received by Landlord: _____

Address: _____

_____

_____

        Authorized signature: _____

Notes: _____

_____

_____

_____

_____

_____

_____

_____

_____

_____

_____

_____

_____

_____

_____

_____

Fixed-Term Residential Lease Agreement

This Lease Agreement is entered into by and between _____
("Landlord"/"Owner"/"Agent"/"Lessor") and _____
("Tenant"/"Resident"/"Lessee") on _____. In the case of multiple Tenants, the Lease Agreement creates joint and several liabilities between Tenants. Landlord and Tenant are collectively the "Parties." Tenant is renting from Landlord property at: _____

_____

_____

("Premises"). This Lease Agreement supersedes any oral or prior written agreement regarding a lease between the Parties. The Parties acknowledge that no representation, inducements, promises, or agreements have been made by or on behalf of any party, except those covenants and agreements in this written agreement. Where context requires, the singular will include the plural, the plural the singular, and genders will include all genders. All Federal, State, and local laws apply where omitted.

In consideration of the mutual promises, the Parties agree as follows:

1. **LEASE AGREEMENT TERM.** The Lease Agreement will begin on _____ and end on _____ as a fixed term tenancy. In accordance with the State Statutes to terminate tenancy the Landlord or Tenant must give the other party a written one (1) months' notice of Lease Agreement non-renewal. The Tenant may only terminate their Lease Agreement on the last day of any month and the Landlord must receive a written notification of non-renewal at least _____days prior to the last day of that month. If the Tenant plans to leave on or after the first of any month, they are responsible for that month's full rent. If the Tenant does not provide the Landlord with a written _____ days' notice, the Tenant will forfeit the full deposit. The vacating Tenant will provide a forwarding address. At the end of the Lease Agreement term date, the tenancy will automatically convert to a month-to-month tenancy until the Tenant gives the Landlord a written one (1) months' notice of Lease Agreement non-renewal. In the event that the Lease Agreement automatically converts to a month-to-month lease, this Lease Agreement will govern the Parties agreement.

2. **LEASE AGREEMENT PAYMENTS.** Tenant agrees to pay Landlord rent for the Premises in the amount of $_____ each month in advance on the 1st day of each month at the following address _____

_____
or at any other address designated by Landlord. If the Lease Agreement Term does not start on the 1st day of the month or end on the last day of a month, the first and last month's rent will be prorated accordingly. Delivery of payment may be paid to _____ by ❑ personal check, ❑ cashier's check, ❑ money order, ❑ _____

3. **LATE CHARGES.** Rent is due on the 1st of each month. If any or all of the rent is not received by the _____day of each month, a $_____ per day late fee charge will be applied until the full rental payment is received. If rent is not received by the date of each month, Tenant will be in breach of the Lease Agreement and eviction proceedings may be initiated.

4. **INSUFFICIENT FUNDS.** Tenant agrees to pay the charge of $_____ for each check ("Bad Check") given by Tenant to Landlord that is returned to Landlord for lack of sufficient funds.

5. **SECURITY DEPOSIT.** At the signing of this Lease Agreement, Tenant will deposit with Landlord, in trust, $_____ "Security Deposit" for the performance by Tenant of the terms under this Lease Agreement, for cleaning the Premises after the Tenant leaves to restore the Premises to the condition it was in prior on the Tenant's arrival, and for damages caused by Tenant, Tenant's family, agents, and visitors to the Premises. The Landlord may use part or all of the Security Deposit to repair damage to the Premises caused by Tenant, Tenant's family, agents, and visitors to the Premises. However, Landlord is not limited to the Security Deposit and Tenant remains liable for any balance. Tenant will not apply or deduct any portion of the Security Deposit for payment of monthly rent, including last month's rent. If Tenant breaches any terms or conditions of this Lease Agreement, Tenant will forfeit any deposit, as permitted by law. Landlord will refund all deposits after deductions, if any, within _____ days after Tenant has vacated the Premises and returned the keys. Keys can be returned to the Landlord or be left on the counter after vacating the Premises. Landlord will provide Tenant an itemization of all Security Deposit deductions.

6. **DEFAULTS.** If Tenant fails to perform or fulfill any obligation under this Lease Agreement, Tenant will be in default of this Lease Agreement. Subject to any State statute, ordinance, or law to the contrary, Tenant will have _____ days from the date of a formal written notice of default by Landlord to cure the default. In the event Tenant does not cure the default, Landlord may, at Landlord's option: a) cure such default and the cost of such action may be added to Tenant's financial obligations under this Lease Agreement; or b) declare Tenant in default of the Lease Agreement. In the event of default, Landlord may also, as permitted by law, re-enter the Premises and re-take possession of the Premises, and Landlord may, at its option, hold Tenant liable for any difference between the rent that would have been payable under this Lease Agreement during the balance of the unexpired term if this Lease Agreement had continued in force and any rent paid by any successive Tenant if the Premises has been re-let. If the Landlord is unable to re-let the Premises during any remaining term of this Lease Agreement, after default by Tenant, Landlord may, at its option, hold Tenant liable for the balance of the unpaid rent under this Lease Agreement if this Lease Agreement had continued in force. The failure of Tenant or their guests or invitees to comply with any term of this Agreement is grounds for termination of the tenancy, with appropriate notice to Tenants and procedures as required by law.

7. **AS-IS CONDITION OF PREMISES.** Tenant agrees to inspect the Premises, including all of the fixtures, the grounds, building, and improvements, and Tenant also acknowledges that the Premises are in good-habitable condition and are habitable. Following an optional walk-through by Tenant, Tenant agrees to accept the Premises in an "As-Is" condition. If at any time during the term of this Lease Agreement, in Tenant's opinion, the conditions change, Tenant will promptly provide reasonable notice to Landlord.

8. **QUIET ENJOYMENT.** Tenant will be entitled to quiet enjoyment of the Premises and Landlord will not interfere with that right, as long as Tenant pays the rent in a timely manner and performs all other obligations under this Lease Agreement.

9. **POSSESSION AND SURRENDER OF PREMISES.** Tenant will be entitled to possession of the

Premises on the 1st day of the Lease Agreement Term. At the expiration of the Lease Agreement, Tenant will peaceably surrender the Premises to the Landlord or Landlord's agent in good condition, as it was at the start of the Lease Agreement, reasonable wear and tear excepted. If, after signing this Lease Agreement, Tenant fails to take possession of the Premises, Tenant will remain responsible for paying rent and complying with all other terms of this Lease Agreement. If Landlord is unable to deliver possession of the Premises to Tenant for any reason not within Landlord's control, including, but not limited to, partial or complete destruction of the Premises, Tenant will have the right to terminate this Agreement upon proper written notice as required by law. In such event, Landlord's liability to Tenant will be limited to the return of all sums previously paid by Tenant to Landlord.

10. **EXCLUSIVE USE AND POSSESSION.** Tenant is given exclusive use and possession of the Premises during the terms of this Lease Agreement for quiet enjoyment as a residence, including all visible areas and closed-door cabinets. If Tenant has exclusive use of an enclosed patio or balcony, the terms extend only to the exclusive enclosed area and do not extend beyond boundaries, nor protrude out of any window or over any fence or balcony railing. The Premises will not be used as any type of business, trade, economic activity, or similar activity for profit or otherwise without prior written consent of Landlord. Tenant will comply with all laws, rules, ordinances, statutes, and orders regarding use of the Premises.

11. **OCCUPANTS.** Tenant agrees that no more than _____ persons may reside on the Premises without prior written consent of the Landlord. Two (2) people per bedroom, plus one (1) additional person e.g., two (2) people may reside in a studio or efficiency Premises, three (3) people in a one (1) bedroom Premises.

12. **ASSIGNMENT AND SUBLEASE.** Tenant ❑ will/ ❑ will not be permitted to assign or sublease any interest in this Lease Agreement. Any sublease arrangement must be made with prior written consent by the Landlord, which consent will not be unreasonably withheld. Any assignment or sublease without Landlord's written prior consent will, at Landlord's option, terminate this Lease Agreement.

13. **PROHIBITION ON LISTING OR ADVERTISING PREMISES ON OVERNIGHT SHORT-TERM SUBLETTING OR RENTING WEBSITES.** The Tenant agrees **NOT** to list or advertise the Premises as available for short-term subletting, rental, or occupancy on Airbnb.com or similar Internet websites. The Tenant agrees that listing or advertising the Premises on Airbnb.com or similar Internet websites is a violation of this Lease Agreement and may be grounds to terminate the Lease Agreement.

14. **PROHIBITION ON SHORT-TERM SUBLETTING OR RENTING.** The Tenant agrees **NOT** to sublet, rent, or allow occupancy by any third party any portion of the Premises. This prohibition applies to overnight stays or any other stay arranged by direct advertising or any Internet listing service, e.g., AirBnB, HomeAway, VRBO, Flipkey, Couchsurfing, Craigslist, Facebook, Instagram, Snapchat, or any other advertising or listing service or other similar Internet sites. Any attempted assignment, whether voluntary or involuntary, at Landlord's election, will constitute a non-curable default. Renting of the Premises through short-term subletting or renting (e.g., Airbnb, or its equivalent), is **NOT** permitted and will be a violation of this Lease Agreement and will be cause for termination of the Lease Agreement and possible loss of the Security Deposit. Any violations of city, county, state, Federal ordinances, or any other regulations related to restrictions on short-term rentals will be forwarded to the proper

authorities.

15. **DANGEROUS MATERIALS.** Tenant will not keep or have on or around the Premises any item of a dangerous, flammable, or explosive nature that may unreasonably increase the risk of fire, explosion, or may be considered hazardous by an insurance company. Tenant is prohibited from creating or allowing excessive smoke to fill the Premises either intentionally, un intentionally, or negligently.

16. **COMBUSTIBLES**. Tenant will not keep or have on or around the Premises gasoline or other combustible materials or permit to do anything that may likely increase the rate of insurance.

17. **UTILITIES ANDS SERVICES.** Tenant will pay all utilities and services, except those included as part of the monthly rent payment and will be paid by the Landlord which are the following that are marked: ❑ gas, ❑ electricity, ❑ water, ❑ sewer, ❑ trash, ❑ heat, ❑ hot water, ❑ internet/wifi, ❑ telephone , ❑ cable, ❑ snow-removal, ❑ lawn, ❑ _____, ❑ _____ , and ❑ _____.

18. **PETS.** Tenant will not keep pets on the Premises without prior written consent of the Landlord. If Landlord grants permission to Tenant to keep a pet, an additional required Pet Security Deposit of $_____will be required by the Landlord to keep in trust for potential damage and cleaning of the Premises. Large aquariums, farm animals, exotic animals, wild animals, and any illegal animals are not permitted on Premises.

19. **WATERBEDS** . Waterbeds are prohibited on the Premises and will be a breach of this Lease Agreement. Tenant will be responsible for any damage caused by non-permissible use of waterbeds.

20. **INVENTORY.** Any furnishings and equipment, if any, provided by the Landlord will be set out in a "Move-In Walk-Through Statement of Condition Supplement for Furnished Premises." An optional "Move-Out Walk-Through Statement of Condition Supplement for Furnished Premises" form will be provided upon moving out.

21. **SMOKING**. Smoking in the Premises of tobacco products, marijuana, and any other substance, legal or illegal, is strictly prohibited. Any violation will be grounds for termination. Any violation of the law will be reported to the proper authorities.

22. **COOKING**. Tenant will not cook or store food items in the Premises, except in the kitchen and the designated food pantry. There is an absolute prohibition to cooking of any nature or fire on the balconies or patios, if any.

23. **MOTORIZED EQUIPMENT**. No motorcycles or equipment driven by a gasoline motor will be permitted inside the Premises.

24. **ILLEGAL DRUGS**. Drug dealing and usage are strictly prohibited and will be reported to the proper authorities without notification to the Tenant. Violations will be grounds for immediate termination of the Lease Agreement, institution of eviction proceedings, and will be forwarded to the appropriate law enforcement authorities where applicable.

25. **ALTERATIONS AND IMPROVEMENTS.** Tenant agrees not to make any improvements or alterations to the Premises without prior written consent of the Landlord. If any alterations, improvement or changes are made to or built on or around the Premises, with the exception

of fixtures and personal property that can be removed without damage to the Premises, will become the property of Landlord and will remain at the end of the Lease Agreement, unless otherwise agreed in writing.

26. **DAMAGE TO PREMISES.** If the Premises or part of the Premises are damaged or destroyed by fire or other casualty not due to Tenant's negligence, the rent will be abated during the time that the Premises are uninhabitable. If Landlord decides not to repair or rebuild the Premises, then this Lease Agreement will terminate and the rent will be prorated up to the time of the damage. Any unearned rent paid in advance will be refunded to Tenant.

27. **PREMISES CLEANLINESS.** Tenant, at the Tenant's sole expense, agrees to keep the Premises clean, particularly in the kitchen, bathrooms, carpets, and floors, including vacuuming regularly, mopping floors, and using household cleaner on hard surfaces. Tenant agrees that it is important to remove dirt and debris that can harbor mold, pests, cause property damage, and interview with the quiet enjoyment of the Premises.

28. **MAINTENANCE AND REPAIR.** Tenant will, at Tenant's sole expense, keep and maintain the Premises in good, clean, and sanitary condition. Tenant will make all repairs to the Premises, fixtures, appliances, and equipment that may have been damaged by Tenant's misuse, waste or neglect, or that of the Tenant's family, agents, visitors, or invitees. Tenant agrees that no painting will be done on the Premises without the prior written consent of Landlord. Tenant will promptly notify Landlord of any damage, defect, or destruction of the Premises or failure of any of the appliances. Landlord will make best efforts to repair or replace any damaged or defective areas, appliances, or equipment that are the Landlord's responsibility to maintain.

29. **RIGHT OF INSPECTION.** Tenant agrees to make the Premises available to Landlord or Landlord's agents for the purposes of inspection, of repairs, of improvements, of services, to show the Premises to prospective buyers or tenants, or in cases of emergency. Except in case of emergency, Landlord will give Tenant reasonable notice of intent to enter. Tenant will not, without Landlord's prior written consent, add, alter or re-key any locks to the Premises. At all times Landlord will be provided with a key or keys capable of unlocking all such locks and gaining entry. Tenant further agrees to notify Landlord in writing if Tenant installs any burglar alarm system, including instructions on how to disarm in cases of emergency.

30. **INSURANCE.** Tenant is required to maintain renter's insurance for the duration of this Lease Agreement. Tenant understands that Landlord will not provide any insurance coverage for Tenant's property. The Landlord's insurance will not be used to cover Tenant's losses. Landlord will not be responsible for any loss of Tenant's property or injuries, whether by theft, fire, riots, strikes, water, smoke, explosion, acts of God or otherwise. All Tenant's must maintain renter's insurance starting on the first day of the rental lease. Proof of renter's insurance will be required at the signing of the Lease Agreement. **Minimum renter's insurance requirements are as follows: $ _____ personal liability and $ _____ personal property coverage.** Tenants may choose an insurance provider of their choice. Tenant must name the Landlord as an interested party on the renter's insurance policy.

31. **NOTICE.** Any notice required or otherwise given pursuant to this Lease Agreement will be in writing. Either Party may change their contact information with a written notice to the other.

32. **NOTIFY LANDLORD.** Tenant will notify the Landlord immediately if there are any issues or

signs of issues with pests, bed bugs, mold, crime, water damage, or any other issue likely to impact health, property, or insurance rates.

33. **WATER LEAKS.** Tenant is to notify the Landlord immediately if Tenant notices any running water in the faucets in the kitchen, bathroom-sink, bathtub or any other faucets that cannot be shut-off through normal use. If the toilet is running and does not cease normally, Tenant is to notify Landlord immediately. If Tenant does not notify Landlord of any water leaks or issues in a reasonable manner, and damage or injuries occur to persons or property due to Tenant's failure to notify the Landlord promptly, Tenant may be held financially responsible for the damage or injuries to persons or property.

34. **DISPLAY OF SIGNS.** Tenant agrees that Tenant will not display any signs on the Premises without the prior written consent of the Landlord. Landlord may display "For Sale", "For Rent", "Vacancy", or similar signs on the Premises and enter to show the Premises to prospective tenants or owners.

35. **NOISE.** Tenant will not cause or allow any unreasonably loud noise or activity in the Premises that may disturb the rights, comforts, conveniences, or quiet enjoyment of other persons. No lounging or visiting will be allowed in the common areas. Furniture delivery and removal will take place between _____ a.m. and _____ p.m.

36. **PARKING.** Tenant will not park on the Premises without the prior written consent of the Landlord and registering of all vehicles with the Landlord. If Landlord grants permission to park on the Premises, Landlord is not responsible for, or assumes liability for, damages caused by fire, theft, casualty, or any other cause with respect to vehicles or its contents.

37. **BALCONIES.** Tenant ❑ will/ ❑ will not use balcony for the purpose of storage, drying clothes, cleaning rugs, or grilling.

38. **LOCKING OF ENTRANCE DOORS.** Landlord reserves the right to close and keep locked all entrance doors of the Premises during such hours as the Landlord deems advisable for the safety and protection of the Premises and its occupants. Tenant will not prop open entrance doors.

39. **EXTENSION OF LEASE.** At the end of this Lease Agreement, the tenancy will automatically convert and continue as a month-to-month lease agreement until the Tenant provides one month's notice to vacate or Landlord provides notice to end the Lease Agreement.

40. **RENT INCREASE.** The Landlord may increase the monthly rent at or after the expiration of the original term of this Lease Agreement by providing the Tenant with written notice at least 30 days prior to the next rent due date. The Tenant then has the option to vacate with proper written notice to the Landlord or remain under the new rental rate and the terms of this Lease Agreement.

41. **HOLDOVER.** In the event Tenant remains in possession of the Premises for any period after the expiration of the Lease Agreement Term ("Holdover Period") a new month-to-month tenancy will be created subject to the same terms and conditions of this Lease Agreement at a monthly rental rate of the same in this Lease Agreement unless otherwise provided by the Landlord in writing. Such month-to-month tenancy will be terminable on thirty (30) days' notice by either Party or on longer notice as required by law.

42. **ABANDONMENT.** If Tenant abandons the Premises of any personal property during the term of this Lease Agreement, Landlord, may at its option, enter the Premises by any legal means without liability to Tenant and may at Landlord's option terminate the Lease Agreement. Abandonment is defined as absence of the Tenants from the Premises for at least _____ consecutive days without notice to Landlord. If Tenant abandons the Premises while the rent is outstanding for more than _____days and there is not reasonable evidence, other than the presence of the Tenants' personal property, that the Tenant is occupying the Premises, Landlord may at Landlord's option terminate this Lease Agreement and regain possession in the manner prescribed by law. Landlord will dispose of all abandoned personal property on the Premises in any manner provided by law. Tenant acknowledges that an abandoned personal property may be disposed at the Tenant's expense as permitted by law.

43. **SEVERABILITY.** If any provision of this Lease Agreement is invalid or unenforceable under applicable law, such provision will be ineffective to the extent of such invalidity or unenforceability only without invalidating or otherwise affecting the remainder of this Lease Agreement. The court will interpret the Lease Agreement in a manner such as to uphold the valid portions of this Agreement while preserving the intent of the Parties.

44. **CUMULATIVE RIGHTS.** Landlord and Tenant rights under this Lease Agreement are cumulative and will not be construed as exclusive of each other unless otherwise required by law.

45. **INDEMNIFICATION.** To the extent permitted by law, Tenant agrees to defend, indemnify, and hold harmless the Landlord from future actions, claims, damages, loss, injuries, attorneys' fees, and costs resulting from the action or inaction of the Tenant, other occupants, and Tenant guests, agents, or invitees in cleaning and maintaining or failure of Tenant to timely report conditions to the Landlord.

46. **VIOLATION OF LEASE AGREEMENT.** Non-compliance of this Lease Agreement will be deemed a material breach of this Lease Agreement and subject to termination by the Landlord.

47. **REMEDY FOR VIOLATION.** Any violation of this Lease Agreement by Tenant constitutes a material breach and allows the Landlord to exercise any default remedies permitted in the Lease Agreement, including termination of the Lease Agreement, in accordance with local laws. Failure to cure a material violation of the Lease Agreement may result in the filing of an Unlawful Detainer (Eviction) action. If an Unlawful Detainer action is filed against the Tenant, it could result in a judgment against the Resident which may include monetary amounts, attorneys' fees, and other court costs. Once a lawsuit is filed with the Court, it may become a public record and may later appear on Tenant's Credit Report which may have an adverse impact on Tenant's Credit Rating. This could seriously affect the Tenant's ability to obtain credit, including future rentals. This clause is not be interpreted to restrict the Landlord's rights to terminate the Lease Agreement for any lawful reason or by any lawful method.

48. **CREDIT REPORTING.** Pursuant to applicable State and Federal law, Tenant is hereby notified that if Tenant does not fulfill the terms of this Lease Agreement, credit obligations, or if Tenant defaults in credit obligations in any way, a negative credit report may be submitted to a credit reporting agency. This is the only notice that Tenant may receive in this regard. Tenant authorizes the Landlord to share any tenancy history or information that the Landlord maintains with other persons or agencies who may inquire as to the Resident's credit or rental history.

49. **MEGAN'S LAW.** Notice: Pursuant to Section 290.46 of the Penal Code, information about specified registered sex offenders is made available to the public via a website maintained by the Department of Justice at www.meganslaw.ca.gov. Depending on an offender's criminal history, this information will include either the address at which the offender resides or the community of residence and ZIP Code in which they reside. (Landlord is NOT required to check this website. If Tenant wants further information, the Landlord recommends that Tenant obtain information from this website prior to signing this Lease Agreement. Landlord does not have expertise in this area. Landlord makes no promises as to its accuracy or obligations to monitor the website.)

50. **COPIES.** Landlord will make copies of this signed Lease Agreement and provide copies to Tenant in a timely manner. Landlord will retain the original wet signatures and make it available for inspection by Tenant upon request. Tenant may request additional copies at any time.

51. **ADDITIONAL TERMS AND CONDITIONS.** _____

_____

_____

_____

_____

_____

52. **TENANT VEHICLE INFORMATION.** Tenant is required to complete a Vehicle Registry and a Parking Addendum for all vehicles on the Premises.

53. **LEAD BASED PAINT DISCLOSURE.**

_____ (Tenant initials) Tenant acknowledges receipt of "Disclosure of Information on Lead-Based Paint or Lead-Based Paint Hazards" from the Landlord.

English version: https://www.epa.gov/sites/production/files/documents/lesr_eng.pdf.

Spanish version: https://www.epa.gov/sites/production/files/documents/spanless.pdf.

_____ (Tenant initials) Tenant acknowledges receipt of pamphlet *Protect Your Family From Lead in Your Home*.

English version: https://www.epa.gov/sites/production/files/documents/selr_eng.pdf.

Spanish version: https://www.epa.gov/sites/production/files/documents/spanless.pdf.

54. **CONTACTS.**

LANDLORD/LANDLORD'S AGENT

Name: _____

Address: _____

_____

Telephone: _____ Email: _____

TENANT

Name: _____

Address: _____

_____

Telephone: _____ Email: _____

TENANT

Name: _____

Address: _____

_____

Telephone: _____ Email: _____

TENANT

Name: _____

Address: _____

_____

Telephone: _____ Email: _____

TENANT

Name: _____

Address: _____

_____

Telephone: _____ Email: _____

IN WITNESS THEREOF, the Parties have caused this Lease Agreement to be executed on the day and year written above. By signing below, the Tenant acknowledges and confirms that he/she has received, reviewed, and understands this Lease Agreement.

_____   _____   _____
Tenant/Lessee (Print)   Tenant/Lessee (Signature)   Date

_____   _____   _____
Tenant/Lessee (Print)   Tenant/Lessee (Signature)   Date

_____   _____   _____
Tenant/Lessee (Print)   Tenant/Lessee (Signature)   Date

_____   _____   _____
Tenant/Lessee (Print)   Tenant/Lessee (Signature)   Date

_____   _____   _____
Landlord/Landlord Agent/Lessor   Landlord/Landlord Agent/Lessor   Date
Agent (Print)   Agent (Signature)

Month-to-Month Residential Lease Agreement

This Lease Agreement is entered into by and between _____ ("Landlord"/"Owner"/"Agent"/"Lessor") and _____ ("Tenant"/"Resident"/"Lessee") on _____. In the case of multiple Tenants, the Lease Agreement creates joint and several liabilities between Tenants. Landlord and Tenant are collectively the "Parties." Tenant is renting from Landlord property at: _____

_____

_____

("Premises"). This Lease Agreement supersedes any oral or prior written agreement regarding a lease between the Parties. The Parties acknowledge that no representation, inducements, promises, or agreements have been made by or on behalf of any party, except those covenants and agreements in this written agreement. Where context requires, the singular will include the plural, the plural the singular, and genders will include all genders. All Federal, State, and local laws apply where omitted.

In consideration of the mutual promises, the Parties agree as follows:

1. **LEASE AGREEMENT TERM.** The Lease Agreement will begin on _____ and end as a month-to-month tenancy. In accordance with the State Statutes to terminate tenancy the Landlord or Tenant must give the other party a written one (1) months' notice of Lease Agreement non-renewal. The Tenant may only terminate their Lease Agreement on the last day of any month and the Landlord must receive a written notification of non-renewal at least _____ days prior to the last day of that month. If the Tenant plans to leave on or after the first of any month, Tenant is responsible for that month's full rent. If Tenant does not provide the Landlord with a written _____ days' notice, Tenant forfeit's the full security deposit. The vacating Tenant will provide a forwarding address.

2. **LEASE AGREEMENT PAYMENTS.** Tenant agrees to pay Landlord rent for the Premises in the amount of $_____ each month in advance on the 1st day of each month at the following address _____

   _____

   or at any other address designated by Landlord. If the Lease Agreement Term does not start on the 1st day of the month or end on the last day of a month, the first and last month's rent will be prorated accordingly. Delivery of payment may be paid to _____ by ❑ personal check, ❑ cashier's check, ❑ money order, ❑ _____

3. **LATE CHARGES.** Rent is due on the 1st of each month. If any or all of the rent is not received by the _____ day of each month, a $_____ per day late fee charge will be applied until the full rental payment is received. If rent is not received by the date of each month, Tenant will be in breach of the Lease Agreement and eviction proceedings may be initiated.

4. **INSUFFICIENT FUNDS.** Tenant agrees to pay the charge of $_____ for each check ("Bad Check") given by Tenant to Landlord that is returned to Landlord for lack of sufficient funds.

5. **SECURITY DEPOSIT.** At the signing of this Lease Agreement, Tenant will deposit with Landlord, in trust, $_____ "Security Deposit" for the performance by Tenant

of the terms under this Lease Agreement, for cleaning the Premises after the Tenant leaves to restore the Premises to the condition it was in prior on the Tenant's arrival, and for damages caused by Tenant, Tenant's family, agents, and visitors to the Premises. The Landlord may use part or all of the Security Deposit to repair damage to the Premises caused by Tenant, Tenant's family, agents, and visitors to the Premises. However, Landlord is not limited to the Security Deposit and Tenant remains liable for any balance. Tenant will not apply or deduct any portion of the Security Deposit for payment of monthly rent, including last month's rent. If Tenant breaches any terms or conditions of this Lease Agreement, Tenant will forfeit any deposit, as permitted by law. Landlord will refund all deposits after deductions, if any, within _____days after Tenant has vacated the Premises and returned the keys. Keys can be returned to the Landlord or be left on the counter after vacating the Premises. Landlord will provide Tenant an itemization of all Security Deposit deductions.

6. **DEFAULTS.** If Tenant fails to perform or fulfill any obligation under this Lease Agreement, Tenant will be in default of this Lease Agreement. Subject to any State statute, ordinance, or law to the contrary, Tenant will have _____days from the date of a formal written notice of default by Landlord to cure the default. In the event Tenant does not cure the default, Landlord may, at Landlord's option: a) cure such default and the cost of such action may be added to Tenant's financial obligations under this Lease Agreement; or b) declare Tenant in default of the Lease Agreement. In the event of default, Landlord may also, as permitted by law, re-enter the Premises and re-take possession of the Premises, and Landlord may, at its option, hold Tenant liable for any difference between the rent that would have been payable under this Lease Agreement during the balance of the unexpired term if this Lease Agreement had continued in force and any rent paid by any successive Tenant if the Premises has been re-let. If the Landlord is unable to re-let the Premises during any remaining term of this Lease Agreement, after default by Tenant, Landlord may, at its option, hold Tenant liable for the balance of the unpaid rent under this Lease Agreement if this Lease Agreement had continued in force. The failure of Tenant or their guests or invitees to comply with any term of this Agreement is grounds for termination of the tenancy, with appropriate notice to Tenants and procedures as required by law.

7. **AS-IS CONDITION OF PREMISES.** Tenant agrees to inspect the Premises, including all of the fixtures, the grounds, building, and improvements, and Tenant also acknowledges that the Premises are in good-habitable condition and are habitable. Following an optional walk-through by Tenant, Tenant agrees to accept the Premises in an "As-Is" condition. If at any time during the term of this Lease Agreement, in Tenant's opinion, the conditions change, Tenant will promptly provide reasonable notice to Landlord.

8. **QUIET ENJOYMENT.** Tenant will be entitled to quiet enjoyment of the Premises and Landlord will not interfere with that right, as long as Tenant pays the rent in a timely manner and performs all other obligations under this Lease Agreement.

9. **POSSESSION AND SURRENDER OF PREMISES.** Tenant will be entitled to possession of the Premises on the 1st day of the Lease Agreement Term. At the expiration of the Lease Agreement, Tenant will peaceably surrender the Premises to the Landlord or Landlord's agent in good condition, as it was at the start of the Lease Agreement, reasonable wear and tear excepted. If, after signing this Lease Agreement, Tenant fails to take possession of the Premises, Tenant will remain responsible for paying rent and complying with all other terms of

this Lease Agreement. If Landlord is unable to deliver possession of the Premises to Tenant for any reason not within Landlord's control, including, but not limited to, partial or complete destruction of the Premises, Tenant will have the right to terminate this Agreement upon proper written notice as required by law. In such event, Landlord's liability to Tenant will be limited to the return of all sums previously paid by Tenant to Landlord.

10. **EXCLUSIVE USE AND POSSESSION.** Tenant is given exclusive use and possession of the Premises during the terms of this Lease Agreement for quiet enjoyment as a residence, including all visible areas and closed-door cabinets. If Tenant has exclusive use of an enclosed patio or balcony, the terms extend only to the exclusive enclosed area and do not extend beyond boundaries, nor protrude out of any window or over any fence or balcony railing. The Premises will not be used as any type of business, trade, economic activity, or similar activity for profit or otherwise without prior written consent of Landlord. Tenant will comply with all laws, rules, ordinances, statutes, and orders regarding use of the Premises.

11. **OCCUPANTS.** Tenant agrees that no more than _____ persons may reside on the Premises without prior written consent of the Landlord. Two (2) people per bedroom, plus one (1) additional person e.g., two (2) people may reside in a studio or efficiency Premises, three (3) people in a one (1) bedroom Premises.

12. **ASSIGNMENT AND SUBLEASE.** Tenant ❏ will/ ❏ will not be permitted to assign or sublease any interest in this Lease Agreement. Any sublease arrangement must be made with prior written consent by the Landlord, which consent will not be unreasonably withheld. Any assignment or sublease without Landlord's written prior consent will, at Landlord's option, terminate this Lease Agreement.

13. **PROHIBITION ON LISTING OR ADVERTISING PREMISES ON OVERNIGHT SHORT-TERM SUBLETTING OR RENTING WEBSITES.** The Tenant agrees **NOT** to list or advertise the Premises as available for short-term subletting, rental, or occupancy on Airbnb.com or similar Internet websites. The Tenant agrees that listing or advertising the Premises on Airbnb.com or similar Internet websites is a violation of this Lease Agreement and may be grounds to terminate the Lease Agreement.

14. **PROHIBITION ON SHORT-TERM SUBLETTING OR RENTING.** The Tenant agrees **NOT** to sublet, rent, or allow occupancy by any third party any portion of the Premises. This prohibition applies to overnight stays or any other stay arranged by direct advertising or any Internet listing service, e.g., AirBnB, HomeAway, VRBO, Flipkey, Couchsurfing, Craigslist, Facebook, Instagram, Snapchat, or any other advertising or listing service or other similar Internet sites. Any attempted assignment, whether voluntary or involuntary, at Landlord's election, will constitute a non-curable default. Renting of the Premises through short-term subletting or renting (e.g., Airbnb, or its equivalent), is **NOT** permitted and will be a violation of this Lease Agreement and will be cause for termination of the Lease Agreement and possible loss of the Security Deposit. Any violations of city, county, state, Federal ordinances, or any other regulations related to restrictions on short-term rentals will be forwarded to the proper authorities.

15. **DANGEROUS MATERIALS.** Tenant will not keep or have on or around the Premises any item of a dangerous, flammable, or explosive nature that may unreasonably increase the risk of fire, explosion, or may be considered hazardous by an insurance company. Tenant is prohibited

from creating or allowing excessive smoke to fill the Premises either intentionally, un intentionally, or negligently.

16. **COMBUSTIBLES**. Tenant will not keep or have on or around the Premises gasoline or other combustible materials or permit to do anything that may likely increase the rate of insurance.

17. **UTILITIES ANDS SERVICES.** Tenant will pay all utilities and services, except those included as part of the monthly rent payment and will be paid by the Landlord which are the following that are marked: ❏ gas, ❏ electricity, ❏ water, ❏ sewer, ❏ trash, ❏ heat, ❏ hot water, ❏ internet/wifi, ❏   telephone , ❏ cable, ❏ snow-removal, ❏ lawn, ❏ _____, ❏ _____, and ❏ _____.

18. **PETS.**   Tenant will not keep pets on the Premises without prior written consent of the Landlord. If Landlord grants permission to Tenant to keep a pet, an additional required Pet Security Deposit of $_____will be required by the Landlord to keep in trust for potential damage and cleaning of the Premises. Large aquariums, farm animals, exotic animals, wild animals, and any illegal animals are not permitted on Premises.

19. **WATERBEDS .** Waterbeds are prohibited on the Premises and will be a breach of this Lease Agreement. Tenant will be responsible for any damage caused by non-permissible use of waterbeds.

20. **INVENTORY.** Any furnishings and equipment, if any, provided by the Landlord will be set out in a "Move-In Walk-Through Statement of Condition Supplement for Furnished Premises." An optional "Move-Out Walk-Through Statement of Condition Supplement for Furnished Premises" form will be provided upon moving out.

21. **SMOKING.** Smoking in the Premises of tobacco products, marijuana, and any other substance, legal or illegal, is strictly prohibited. Any violation will be grounds for termination. Any violation of the law will be reported to the proper authorities.

22. **COOKING**. Tenant will not cook or store food items in the Premises, except in the kitchen and the designated food pantry. There is an absolute prohibition to cooking of any nature or fire on the balconies or patios, if any.

23. **MOTORIZED EQUIPMENT**. No motorcycles or equipment driven by a gasoline motor will be permitted inside the Premises.

24. **ILLEGAL DRUGS**. Drug dealing and usage are strictly prohibited and will be reported to the proper authorities without notification to the Tenant.   Violations will be grounds for immediate termination of the Lease Agreement, institution of eviction proceedings, and will be forwarded to the appropriate law enforcement authorities where applicable.

25. **ALTERATIONS AND IMPROVEMENTS.**   Tenant agrees not to make any improvements or alterations to the Premises without prior written consent of the Landlord. If any alterations, improvement or changes are made to or built on or around the Premises, with the exception of fixtures and personal property that can be removed without damage to the Premises, will become the property of Landlord and will remain at the end of the Lease Agreement, unless otherwise agreed in writing.

26. **DAMAGE TO PREMISES.**   If the Premises or part of the Premises are damaged or destroyed by

fire or other casualty not due to Tenant's negligence, the rent will be abated during the time that the Premises are uninhabitable. If Landlord decides not to repair or rebuild the Premises, then this Lease Agreement will terminate and the rent will be prorated up to the time of the damage. Any unearned rent paid in advance will be refunded to Tenant.

27. **PREMISES CLEANLINESS.** Tenant, at the Tenant's sole expense, agrees to keep the Premises clean, particularly in the kitchen, bathrooms, carpets, and floors, including vacuuming regularly, mopping floors, and using household cleaner on hard surfaces. Tenant agrees that it is important to remove dirt and debris that can harbor mold, pests, cause property damage, and interview with the quiet enjoyment of the Premises.

28. **MAINTENANCE AND REPAIR.** Tenant will, at Tenant's sole expense, keep and maintain the Premises in good, clean, and sanitary condition. Tenant will make all repairs to the Premises, fixtures, appliances, and equipment that may have been damaged by Tenant's misuse, waste or neglect, or that of the Tenant's family, agents, visitors, or invitees. Tenant agrees that no painting will be done on the Premises without the prior written consent of Landlord. Tenant will promptly notify Landlord of any damage, defect, or destruction of the Premises or failure of any of the appliances. Landlord will make best efforts to repair or replace any damaged or defective areas, appliances, or equipment that are the Landlord's responsibility to maintain.

29. **RIGHT OF INSPECTION.** Tenant agrees to make the Premises available to Landlord or Landlord's agents for the purposes of inspection, of repairs, of improvements, of services, to show the Premises to prospective buyers or tenants, or in cases of emergency. Except in case of emergency, Landlord will give Tenant reasonable notice of intent to enter. Tenant will not, without Landlord's prior written consent, add, alter or re-key any locks to the Premises. At all times Landlord will be provided with a key or keys capable of unlocking all such locks and gaining entry. Tenant further agrees to notify Landlord in writing if Tenant installs any burglar alarm system, including instructions on how to disarm in cases of emergency.

30. **INSURANCE.** Tenant is required to maintain renter's insurance for the duration of this Lease Agreement. Tenant understands that Landlord will not provide any insurance coverage for Tenant's property. The Landlord's insurance will not be used to cover Tenant's losses. Landlord will not be responsible for any loss of Tenant's property or injuries, whether by theft, fire, riots, strikes, water, smoke, explosion, acts of God or otherwise. All Tenant's must maintain renter's insurance starting on the first day of the rental lease. Proof of renter's insurance will be required at the signing of the Lease Agreement. **Minimum renter's insurance requirements are as follows: $ _____ personal liability and $ _____ personal property coverage.** Tenants may choose an insurance provider of their choice. Tenant must name the Landlord as an interested party on the renter's insurance policy.

31. **NOTICE.** Any notice required or otherwise given pursuant to this Lease Agreement will be in writing. Either Party may change their contact information with a written notice to the other.

32. **NOTIFY LANDLORD.** Tenant will notify the Landlord immediately if there are any issues or signs of issues with pests, bed bugs, mold, crime, water damage, or any other issue likely to impact health, property, or insurance rates.

33. **WATER LEAKS.** Tenant is to notify the Landlord immediately if Tenant notices any running water in the faucets in the kitchen, bathroom-sink, bathtub or any other faucets that cannot

be shut-off through normal use. If the toilet is running and does not cease normally, Tenant is to notify Landlord immediately. If Tenant does not notify Landlord of any water leaks or issues in a reasonable manner, and damage or injuries occur to persons or property due to Tenant's failure to notify the Landlord promptly, Tenant may be held financially responsible for the damage or injuries to persons or property.

34. **DISPLAY OF SIGNS.** Tenant agrees that Tenant will not display any signs on the Premises without the prior written consent of the Landlord. Landlord may display "For Sale", "For Rent", "Vacancy", or similar signs on the Premises and enter to show the Premises to prospective tenants or owners.

35. **NOISE.** Tenant will not cause or allow any unreasonably loud noise or activity in the Premises that may disturb the rights, comforts, conveniences, or quiet enjoyment of other persons. No lounging or visiting will be allowed in the common areas. Furniture delivery and removal will take place between _____ a.m. and _____ p.m.

36. **PARKING.** Tenant will not park on the Premises without the prior written consent of the Landlord and registering of all vehicles with the Landlord. If Landlord grants permission to park on the Premises, Landlord is not responsible for, or assumes liability for, damages caused by fire, theft, casualty, or any other cause with respect to vehicles or its contents.

37. **BALCONIES.** Tenant ❏ will/ ❏ will not use balcony for the purpose of storage, drying clothes, cleaning rugs, or grilling.

38. **LOCKING OF ENTRANCE DOORS.** Landlord reserves the right to close and keep locked all entrance doors of the Premises during such hours as the Landlord deems advisable for the safety and protection of the Premises and its occupants. Tenant will not prop open entrance doors.

39. **EXTENSION OF LEASE.** At the end of this Lease Agreement, the tenancy will automatically convert and continue as a month-to-month lease agreement until the Tenant provides one month's notice to vacate or Landlord provides notice to end the Lease Agreement.

40. **RENT INCREASE.** The Landlord may increase the monthly rent at or after the expiration of the original term of this Lease Agreement by providing the Tenant with written notice at least 30 days prior to the next rent due date. The Tenant then has the option to vacate with proper written notice to the Landlord or remain under the new rental rate and the terms of this Lease Agreement.

41. **HOLDOVER.** In the event Tenant remains in possession of the Premises for any period after the expiration of the Lease Agreement Term ("Holdover Period") a new month-to-month tenancy will be created subject to the same terms and conditions of this Lease Agreement at a monthly rental rate of the same in this Lease Agreement unless otherwise provided by the Landlord in writing. Such month-to-month tenancy will be terminable on thirty (30) days' notice by either Party or on longer notice as required by law.

42. **ABANDONMENT.** If Tenant abandons the Premises of any personal property during the term of this Lease Agreement, Landlord, may at its option, enter the Premises by any legal means without liability to Tenant and may at Landlord's option terminate the Lease Agreement. Abandonment is defined as absence of the Tenants from the Premises for at least _____

consecutive days without notice to Landlord. If Tenant abandons the Premises while the rent is outstanding for more than _____days and there is not reasonable evidence, other than the presence of the Tenants' personal property, that the Tenant is occupying the Premises, Landlord may at Landlord's option terminate this Lease Agreement and regain possession in the manner prescribed by law. Landlord will dispose of all abandoned personal property on the Premises in any manner provided by law. Tenant acknowledges that an abandoned personal property may be disposed at the Tenant's expense as permitted by law.

43. **SEVERABILITY.** If any provision of this Lease Agreement is invalid or unenforceable under applicable law, such provision will be ineffective to the extent of such invalidity or unenforceability only without invalidating or otherwise affecting the remainder of this Lease Agreement. The court will interpret the Lease Agreement in a manner such as to uphold the valid portions of this Agreement while preserving the intent of the Parties.

44. **CUMULATIVE RIGHTS.** Landlord and Tenant rights under this Lease Agreement are cumulative and will not be construed as exclusive of each other unless otherwise required by law.

45. **INDEMNIFICATION.** To the extent permitted by law, Tenant agrees to defend, indemnify, and hold harmless the Landlord from future actions, claims, damages, loss, injuries, attorneys' fees, and costs resulting from the action or inaction of the Tenant, other occupants, and Tenant guests, agents, or invitees in cleaning and maintaining or failure of Tenant to timely report conditions to the Landlord.

46. **VIOLATION OF LEASE AGREEMENT.** Non-compliance of this Lease Agreement will be deemed a material breach of this Lease Agreement and subject to termination by the Landlord.

47. **REMEDY FOR VIOLATION.** Any violation of this Lease Agreement by Tenant constitutes a material breach and allows the Landlord to exercise any default remedies permitted in the Lease Agreement, including termination of the Lease Agreement, in accordance with local laws. Failure to cure a material violation of the Lease Agreement may result in the filing of an Unlawful Detainer (Eviction) action. If an Unlawful Detainer action is filed against the Tenant, it could result in a judgment against the Resident which may include monetary amounts, attorneys' fees, and other court costs. Once a lawsuit is filed with the Court, it may become a public record and may later appear on Tenant's Credit Report which may have an adverse impact on Tenant's Credit Rating. This could seriously affect the Tenant's ability to obtain credit, including future rentals. This clause is not be interpreted to restrict the Landlord's rights to terminate the Lease Agreement for any lawful reason or by any lawful method.

48. **CREDIT REPORTING.** Pursuant to applicable State and Federal law, Tenant is hereby notified that if Tenant does not fulfill the terms of this Lease Agreement, credit obligations, or if Tenant defaults in credit obligations in any way, a negative credit report may be submitted to a credit reporting agency. This is the only notice that Tenant may receive in this regard. Tenant authorizes the Landlord to share any tenancy history or information that the Landlord maintains with other persons or agencies who may inquire as to the Resident's credit or rental history.

49. **MEGAN'S LAW.** Notice: Pursuant to Section 290.46 of the Penal Code, information about specified registered sex offenders is made available to the public via a website maintained by the Department of Justice at www.meganslaw.ca.gov. Depending on an offender's criminal history, this information will include either the address at which the offender resides or the

community of residence and ZIP Code in which they reside. (Landlord is NOT required to check this website. If Tenant wants further information, the Landlord recommends that Tenant obtain information from this website prior to signing this Lease Agreement. Landlord does not have expertise in this area. Landlord makes no promises as to its accuracy or obligations to monitor the website.)

50. **COPIES.** Landlord will make copies of this signed Lease Agreement and provide copies to Tenant in a timely manner. Landlord will retain the original wet signatures and make it available for inspection by Tenant upon request. Tenant may request additional copies at any time.

51. **ADDITIONAL TERMS AND CONDITIONS.** _____

_____

_____

_____

_____

_____

_____

_____

_____

52. **TENANT VEHICLE INFORMATION.** Tenant is required to complete a Vehicle Registry and a Parking Addendum for all vehicles on the Premises.

53. **LEAD BASED PAINT DISCLOSURE**.

_____ (Tenant initials) Tenant acknowledges receipt of "Disclosure of Information on Lead-Based Paint or Lead-Based Paint Hazards" from the Landlord.

English version: https://www.epa.gov/sites/production/files/documents/lesr_eng.pdf.

Spanish version: https://www.epa.gov/sites/production/files/documents/spanless.pdf.

_____ (Tenant initials) Tenant acknowledges receipt of pamphlet *Protect Your Family From Lead in Your Home*.

English version: https://www.epa.gov/sites/production/files/documents/selr_eng.pdf.

Spanish version: https://www.epa.gov/sites/production/files/documents/spanless.pdf.

54. **CONTACTS.**

LANDLORD/LANDLORD'S AGENT

Name: _____

Address: _____

_____

Telephone: _____ Email: _____

TENANT

Name: _____

Address: _____

_____

Telephone: _____ Email: _____

TENANT

Name: _____

Address: _____

_____

Telephone: _____ Email: _____

TENANT

Name: _____

Address: _____

_____

Telephone: _____ Email: _____

TENANT

Name: _____

Address: _____

_____

Telephone: _____ Email: _____

IN WITNESS THEREOF, the Parties have caused this Lease Agreement to be executed on the day and year written above. By signing below, the Tenant acknowledges and confirms that he/she has received, reviewed, and understands this Lease Agreement.

_____   _____   _____
Tenant/Lessee (Print)   Tenant/Lessee (Signature)   Date

_____   _____   _____
Tenant/Lessee (Print)   Tenant/Lessee (Signature)   Date

_____   _____   _____
Tenant/Lessee (Print)   Tenant/Lessee (Signature)   Date

_____   _____   _____
Tenant/Lessee (Print)   Tenant/Lessee (Signature)   Date

_____   _____   _____
Landlord/Landlord Agent/Lessor   Landlord/Landlord Agent/Lessor   Date
Agent (Print)   Agent (Signature)

Self-Storage Addendum to Lease Agreement

This Addendum is entered into by and between _____, "Lessor"

and _____, "Lessee."

Lessee is renting from Lessor the Premises located at: _____

_____

This Addendum is incorporated into the Lease Agreement between Lessor and Lessee, and this Addendum controls in the event of conflict with the Lease Agreement. The term of this Addendum will begin on the commencement date set forth in this Addendum and end on the expiration date set forth in the Lease Agreement unless otherwise provided in this Addendum or subsequent writing(s). This Addendum supersedes all oral and prior written agreements regarding self-storage. The Parties acknowledge that no representation, inducements, promises, or agreements have been made by or on behalf of any party, except those covenants and agreements in this written agreement. Where context requires, the singular will include the plural, the plural the singular, and genders will include all genders. All Federal, State, and local laws apply where omitted. In consideration of the mutual promises, Lessor and Lessee agree as follows:

In accordance with Federal, State, and local laws covering Self-Storage Areas, no flammable materials, perishables, illegal substances, or articles that may be dangerous to the Lessor, Lessee, any persons or animals, to the Premises, or that may cause an increase in insurance premiums may be stored in the Premises. Any items found to be in violation may be removed by the Lessor at Lessee's expense.

1. The Self-Storage Area is described (e.g., square feet, shape) as follows: _____

    _____

    _____

    _____

2. Lessee will provide at least a 30-day notice in writing of intent to cancel or not renew this agreement.

3. Lessor will be under no obligation to renew or extend this Agreement.

4. The Lessee agrees that at expiration of this Agreement, he/she will remove all items from the Self-Storage Area and leave the area "broom clean."

5. Lessor will take possession of the Self-Storage Area immediately on termination of this Agreement and reserve the right to remove any materials stored therein.

6. Lessor will have the right to take possession of the Self-Storage Area when the rent for the space will not have been paid by the 15th of the month, then due.

7. Lessor may remove any contents found therein and sell the contents to satisfy delinquent rents after the Lessor has taken possession of the Self-Storage Area.

8. The Lessor may revoke the Lessee's self-storage privileges in case of violation of this Agreement, default on rental payments, or violations of the Lease Agreement.

9. Lessor will provide Lessee with a key that is issued and controlled by the Lessor.

10. Lessee will not have the right to assign use of the Self-Storage Area to a third-party.

11. Lessor will not release keys without the expressed written consent of the Lessee.

12. Lessee will not have the right to make any modifications, alterations, renovations, wall additions, wall removals, electrical, plumbing, etc. to the Self-Storage Area or Premises.

13. It is the responsibility of the Lessee to notify the Lessor immediately of any leaks or power outages within the Self-Storage Area.

14. A valid, non-expired government issued, photo identification card must be presented to the Lessor prior to signing this Agreement or keys being issued.

15. Lessor may limit use or access to the Premises to facilitate necessary maintenance.

16. Lessor will have the right to enter the Premises without the written or verbal consent of the Lessee for the purposes of inspection for reasonable suspicion of violations of this Agreement or laws, of making repairs or improvements, to show the Self-Storage Area to prospective buyers or tenants (after written notice to Lessee as permitted by law), or in cases of emergency (e.g., fire, flood, acts of God).

17. Lessee agrees to release the Self-Storage Area at the expiration of this Agreement, end of the Lease Agreement, acts that are in violation of this Agreement or law that require the Lessor to take possession, abandonment of the Premises, and acts which present a hazard to persons, property, or likely to increase insurance rates.

18. Lessee is cautioned against storing items of high monetary or sentimental value in the Self-Storage Area. Items are stored at the Lessee's sole risk and labor. It is understood that the Lessee is not responsible for lost, stolen, damaged, or discarded items.

19. Lessee retains the right to inspect the Premises and the Self-Storage Area as permitted by law.

20. Lessee retains the right to terminate this agreement of the self-storage unit with or without cause.

By signing below, Lessee(s) acknowledge and confirm that he/she has received, reviewed, and understands this Addendum.

_____   _____   _____   _____
Lessee   Date   Lessee   Date

_____   _____   _____   _____
Lessee   Date   Lessee   Date

_____   _____   _____   _____
Lessor   Date   Lessor   Date

_____   _____   _____   _____
Lessor Agent   Date   Lessor Agent   Date

Renter's Insurance Requirements

Tenant(s) Name(s): _____

Address: _____

_____

The Landlord does <u>NOT</u> maintain insurance to cover the personal liability or personal property of tenant(s) or their guest(s) or occupant(s). Resident must maintain renter's insurance starting on the first day of the rental lease. Proof of renter's insurance is required at lease signing. Resident's may choose an insurance provider of their choice. All Federal, State, and local laws apply where omitted. As a condition of the lease, residents are required to:

1. Maintain and provide proof of coverage for a minimum of $_____ personal liability and $_____ in personal property coverage prior to move-in.

2. Resident's must list: _____ as an "Interested Party" on the declaration page with the insurance company so the insurance company will notify the Landlord in the event of a cancellation or change in the policy.

3. WATER COVERAGE MUST BE PROVIDED FOR NEGLIGENT RESIDENT-CAUSED DAMAGE TO THE INSURED'S PREMISES AS WELL AS ADJACENT UNITS DAMAGED DUE TO THE INSURED'S NEGLIGENT ACTIONS (i.e., if Tenant accidentally overflows the bathtub).

**At least one of the boxes below must be completed.

Insurance Agent Acknowledgement: As the insurance agent for the resident, I understand the above stated conditions and certify that the renter's insurance policy provided to the insured by my agency contains coverage that satisfies these stated minimum renter's insurance lease requirements.

Agency Name: _____

Signature: _____   Date: _____

Resident Acknowledgement: I understand that by not obtaining my insurance agent's signature of coverage certification above, I acknowledge and agree to the minimum renter's insurance lease requirements. Furthermore, I agree that if my policy does not provide coverage that meets these requirements, I am fully responsible for any negligence damage caused to the Landlord's property not covered by my insurance policy.

Signature: _____   Date: _____

_____   _____
Tenant/Lessee (Signature)   Date   Tenant/Lessee (Signature)   Date

_____   _____
Tenant/Lessee (Signature)   Date   Tenant/Lessee (Signature)   Date

Pet Addendum to Lease Agreement

This Addendum is entered into by and between _____,

"Owner/Agent" and _____, "Resident."

Resident is renting from Owner the "Premises" located at: _____

_____

This Addendum is incorporated into the Lease Agreement between Lessor and Lessee, and this Addendum controls in the event of conflict with the Lease Agreement. The term of this Addendum will begin on the commencement date set forth in this Addendum and end on the expiration date set forth in the Lease Agreement unless otherwise provided in this Addendum or subsequent writing(s). This Addendum supersedes all oral and prior written agreements regarding pets. The Parties acknowledge that no representation, inducements, promises, or agreements have been made by or on behalf of any party, except those covenants and agreements in this written agreement. Where context requires, the singular will include the plural, the plural the singular, and genders all genders. All Federal, State, and local laws apply where omitted. In consideration of the mutual promises, Owner and Resident agree as follows:

❑ Pets are NOT allowed in the Premises for overnight, long-term, or short-term stays .

❑ Pets are allowed only with prior written consent. No more than _____ pets in total are allowed. The Resident will be asked to remove, at the Owner's sole discretion, any pet that disturbs residents, whether the pet is inside or outside the Premises or constitutes a problem or obstruction to the Owner. Any damage in excess of the Pet Security Deposit and Security Deposit will be the responsibility of the Resident. A photo of each pet taken within the last three months is required.

    ❑ Dogs require liability insurance prior to dogs being brought onto the Premise. Dogs have a Pet Security Deposit fee of $_____ which is ❑ refundable/ ❑ non-refundable. An ongoing monthly pet rental fee of $_____ per dog is required. The combined weight limit of all of the dogs, breeds, and total number of dogs are restricted; please check with Owner. The Resident agrees to purchase and maintain a pet owner's insurance that lists the Owner as an "Interested Party."

    ❑ Cats have an upfront fee of $_____ which is ❑ refundable/ ❑ non-refundable. An ongoing monthly pet rental fee of $_____ per cat is required. The total number of cats are restricted; please check with Owner.

❑ Other animals (e.g., fish, birds, hamsters) require prior approval and fees. Large aquariums that hold more than 20 gallons of water are not permitted .

_____	_____	_____	_____
Resident/Lessee	Date	Resident/Lessee	Date
_____	_____	_____	_____
Resident/Lessee	Date	Resident/Lessee	Date
_____	_____	_____	_____
Owner/Agent/Lessor	Date	Owner/Agent/Lessor	Date

Parking Addendum to Lease Agreement

This Addendum is entered into by and between _____,

"Owner/Agent" and _____, "Resident."

Resident is renting from Owner the "Premises" located at: _____

_____

This Addendum is incorporated into the Lease Agreement between Lessor and Lessee, and this Addendum controls in the event of conflict with the Lease Agreement. The term of this Addendum will begin on the commencement date set forth in this Addendum and end on the expiration date set forth in the Lease Agreement unless otherwise provided in this Addendum or subsequent writing(s). This Addendum supersedes all oral and prior written agreements regarding parking. The Parties acknowledge that no representation, inducements, promises, or agreements have been made by or on behalf of any party, except those covenants and agreements in this written agreement. Where context requires, the singular will include the plural, the plural the singular, and genders will include all genders. All Federal, State, and local laws apply where omitted. In consideration of the mutual promises, Owner and Resident agree as follows:

1. Parking is assigned as follows:

    ❑   Free parking is provided for _____ number of vehicles.   ❑   Additional vehicles will be provided for a monthly fee of $ _____. Parking payments are due on the same schedule as rent payments.

    ❑   Parking is provided for a monthly fee of $ _____. Parking payments are due on the same schedule as rent payments.

    ❑   Additional unassigned street parking is available

2. Vehicles parked on the Premises must be registered to Resident and maintain current State vehicle registration tags. The license plate number, make, and model of the vehicle are required to be disclosed to the Owner. Also, a copy of the Resident's State-issued Driver's license will be required. All vehicles on Premises must be registered with Owner. Cars, trucks, boats, trailers, motorcycles, recreational vehicles, or commercial vehicles are prohibited on the Premises without the express prior written consent of the Owner.

3. Residents are required to keep the Owner informed of vehicle license numbers of any vehicles that will be parked on the Premises.

4. Parking permits, if provided, are to be properly displayed at all times.

5. Vehicle maintenance, upkeep, and/or repairs are **NOT** permitted on the Premises. No car parts, broken or disabled vehicles are stored on the Premises or anywhere else on the Premises. Non-operative vehicles will be towed at Resident's expense. No trailers, boats, campers, recreational vehicles, or trucks over one ton are allowed without prior written authorization. Prohibited activities include, but are not limited to, carwashes, painting, repairs of any kind, and oil changes.

6. The parking areas are not for storage. Combustible, hazardous, explosive materials, or dangerous accumulations of rubbish, wastepaper, boxes, shavings, or any highly flammable materials is not

permitted as this is a fire violation and safety hazard.

7. Garage doors, if any, must be kept closed. WARNING: rain and moisture can cause a garage door to shut unexpectedly due to added weight. Please be aware of this possibility and advise the Owner if you notice any problem with the operation of any garage doors.

8. All cars are to be kept in a clean, orderly, and operative condition. Vehicles with $500.00 or more in damages as a result of an accident or otherwise, flat tires, non-operational vehicles, and vehicles left in the same spot for over 72 hours are subject to immediate tow at the expense of the vehicle owner.

9. Vehicle leaks are strictly prohibited and may be the basis for the termination of this Addendum or Lease Agreement. The Resident agrees to pay the Owner a fee of $ 100.00 for every occurrence where the Owner must, as determined at the Owner's sole discretion, clean oil or other fluids from the Premises due to any leaks from any vehicles owned or operated by the Resident, their household, guests, invitees, or agents.

10. Owner reserves the right to prohibit any vehicle on the Premises, including oversized vehicles and vehicles with altered or modified mufflers or exhaust systems whereby the noise level is judged by the Owner or its agents to constitute a nuisance or disturbance to others, or any other vehicle displaying anything potentially offensive.

11. Vehicles not registered with the Owner are in violation of this Addendum and whether legally or illegally parked, will be towed away at the Vehicle owner's expense. Parking in designated fire lanes, double parking, or parking on the grass is prohibited, and violators may be towed at the vehicle owner's expense.

Comments: _____

_____

_____

_____

_____

_____

_____

By signing below, Resident confirms that he/she has received, reviewed, and understands this Addendum.

_____	_____	_____	_____
Resident/Lessee	Date	Resident/Lessee	Date
_____	_____	_____	_____
Resident/Lessee	Date	Resident/Lessee	Date
_____	_____	_____	_____
Owner/Lessor or Owner Agent/ Lessor Agent	Date	Owner/Lessor or Owner Agent/ Lessor Agent	Date

Vehicle Registration

Resident(s) Name(s): _____

_____

Address: _____

_____

Number of Authorized Vehicles: _____

☐ Year, Make, Model, and Color: _____

    License Plate #/State: _____/_____ Permit #: _____ Space #: _____

☐ Year, Make, Model, and Color: _____

    License Plate #/State: _____/_____ Permit #: _____ Space #: _____

☐ Year, Make, Model, and Color: _____

    License Plate #/State: _____/_____ Permit #: _____ Space #: _____

☐ Year, Make, Model, and Color: _____

    License Plate #/State: _____/_____ Permit #: _____ Space #: _____

I understand that I am only to park in my designated space(s) to which I am been assigned. I agree not to park illegally. Cancellation of an assigned parking space must be submitted in writing 30 days in advance. The Landlord cannot be held responsible for damage to vehicles or their contents for any reason, including due to theft, fire, water, smoke, explosion, acts of God, or otherwise.

Comments: _____

_____

_____

_____

_____

_____

_____

_____

_____

_____

_____

_____

Key Release Addendum to Lease Agreement

This Addendum is entered into by and between _____,

"Owner/Agent" and _____, "Resident."

Resident is renting from Owner the "Premises" located at: _____

_____

This Addendum is incorporated into the Lease Agreement between Lessor and Lessee, and this Addendum controls in the event of conflict with the Lease Agreement. The term of this Addendum will begin on the commencement date set forth in this Addendum and end on the expiration date set forth in the Lease Agreement unless otherwise provided in this Addendum or subsequent writing(s). This Addendum supersedes all oral and prior written agreements regarding key release. The Parties acknowledge that no representation, inducements, promises, or agreements have been made by or on behalf of any party, except those covenants and agreements in this written agreement. Where context requires, the singular will include the plural, the plural the singular, and genders will include all genders. All Federal, State, and local laws apply where omitted. Resident has been assigned the following keys providing access to the residence, garage, gates, and/or common areas:

❑ Front door number of keys: _____   ❑ Mailbox   ❑ Remote

❑ Other: _____   ❑ Other: _____   ❑ Other: _____

All keys issued to the Resident must be returned to the Owner upon move-out by giving keys to the Owner or by leaving the keys on the counter.

Resident agree to notify the Owner of any lost or stolen keys. There will be a fee of $_____ for each lost key and $_____ for each remote not returned on move-out.

In the event the Resident is locked out of the Premises for any reason other than by the Owner, the Resident agrees to pay $ _____ to the Owner for providing entry into the Premises if such entry is made other than during normal business hours.

Comments: _____

_____

_____

By signing below, Resident confirms that he/she has received, reviewed, and understands this Addendum.

_____   _____   _____   _____
Resident/Lessee   Date   Resident/Lessee   Date

_____   _____   _____   _____
Resident/Lessee   Date   Resident/Lessee   Date

_____   _____   _____   _____
Owner/Lessor or Owner Agent/   Date   Owner/Lessor or Owner Agent/   Date
Lessor Agent   Lessor Agent

Prohibition Against Short-Term Subletting or Renting Addendum to Lease Agreement

This Addendum is entered into by and between _____,

"Owner/Agent" and _____, "Resident."

Resident is renting from Owner the "Premises" located at: _____

_____

This Addendum is incorporated into the Lease Agreement between Lessor and Lessee, and this Addendum controls in the event of conflict with the Lease Agreement. The term of this Addendum will begin on the commencement date set forth in this Addendum and end on the expiration date set forth in the Lease Agreement unless otherwise provided in this Addendum or subsequent writing(s). This Addendum supersedes all oral and prior written agreements regarding short-term subletting or renting. The Parties acknowledge that no representation, inducements, promises, or agreements have been made by or on behalf of any party, except those covenants and agreements in this written agreement. Where context requires, the singular will include the plural, the plural the singular, and genders will include all genders. All Federal, State, and local laws apply where omitted. In consideration of the mutual promises, Owner and Resident agree as follows:

Renting out of the Premises through short-term subletting or renting (e.g., Airbnb, or its equivalent), is **NOT** permitted. Any violations will be cause for termination of the Lease Agreement and possible loss of Security Deposit. Also, any violations of city, county, State, and Federal ordinances or other regulations related to restrictions on short-term rentals will be forwarded to the proper authorities.

SHORT-TERM SUBLETTING OR RENTING IS PROHIBITED. The Resident is strictly prohibited from subletting or renting to any third party, or allowing occupancy by any third party, or all or any portion of the leased Premises, whether for an overnight use or duration of any length. This prohibition applies to overnight stays or any other stays arranged by direct advertising or any Internet listing service, e.g., AirBnB, HomeAway, VRBO, Flipkey, Couchsurfing, Craigslist, Facebook, Instagram, Snapchat, or any other advertising or listing service. Any attempted assignment, whether voluntary or involuntary, will constitute a non-curable violation of this Addendum.

PROHIBITION ON LISTING OR ADVERTISING PREMISES ON OVERNIGHT SUBLETTING OR RENTING WEBSITES. The Resident agrees not to list or advertise the Premises as being available for short-term subletting or rental or occupancy by others on Airbnb.com or similar Internet websites. The Resident agrees that listing or advertising the Premises on Airbnb.com or similar Internet websites is a violation of this Addendum.

VIOLATION OF LEASE AGREEMENT. The Premises are to be used solely as a private residence and strictly prohibits conducting any kind of business in, from, or involving the Premises, unless expressly permitted by law or by prior written consent by the Owner. In addition, subletting or allowing others occupancy the Premises for any period of time without prior written consent by the Owner is prohibited. Permitting the Premises to be used for any subletting or rental or occupancy by others (including, without limitation, for a short-term), regardless of the value of consideration received, if any, is a violation of this Addendum.

REMEDY FOR VIOLATION. Any violation of this Addendum constitutes a material breach of the Lease Agreement and allows the Owner to exercise any default remedies permitted in the Lease Agreement, including termination of the Lease Agreement, in accordance with local and State laws. Failure to cure a material breach of the Lease Agreement may result in the filing of an Unlawful Detainer (Eviction) action against the Resident. If an Unlawful Detainer action is filed against the Resident, it could result in a judgment against the Resident which may include monetary amounts, attorneys' fees, and other court costs. Once a lawsuit is filed with the Court, it may become a public record and may later appear on the Resident's Credit Report and may have an adverse impact on the Resident's Credit Rating. This could seriously affect the Resident's ability to obtain future credit, including future rentals. This clause is not be interpreted to restrict the Owner's rights to terminate the Lease Agreement for any lawful reason.

RESIDENT LIABILITY. The Resident is responsible and liable for any and all losses, damages, and fines that the Owner incurs as a result of the Resident's violations of the terms of this Addendum. Further, the Resident agrees that the Resident is responsible for and will be held liable for any and all actions of any persons who occupy the Premises in violation of the terms of this Addendum, e.g., property damage, disturbance of other residents, violence, and attempted violence on another person. In accordance with applicable laws, without limiting the Resident's liability, the Resident agrees the Owner will have the right to collect against any renter's or liability insurance policy maintained by the Renter for any losses or damages that the Owner incurs as the result of any violations of this Addendum.

SEVERABILITY. If any provision of this Addendum is invalid or unenforceable under applicable law, such provision will be ineffective to the extent of such invalidity or unenforceability only without invalidating or otherwise affecting the remainder of this Addendum. The court will interpret this Addendum and provisions in a manner as to uphold the valid portions of this Addendum while preserving the intent of the Parties.

Comments: _____

_____

_____

_____

_____

_____

_____

_____

By signing below, Resident confirms that he/she has received, reviewed, and understands this Addendum.

Resident/Lessee	Date	Resident/Lessee	Date
Resident/Lessee	Date	Resident/Lessee	Date
Owner/Lessor or Owner Agent/ Lessor Agent	Date	Owner/Lessor or Owner Agent/ Lessor Agent	Date

Package Pick-Up Addendum to Lease Agreement

This Addendum is entered into by and between _____,
"Owner/Agent" and _____, "Resident."

Resident is renting from Owner the "Premises" located at: _____
_____

This Addendum is incorporated into the Lease Agreement between Lessor and Lessee, and this Addendum controls in the event of conflict with the Lease Agreement. The term of this Addendum will begin on the commencement date set forth in this Addendum and end on the expiration date set forth in the Lease Agreement unless otherwise provided in this Addendum or subsequent writing(s). This Addendum supersedes all oral and prior written agreements regarding package pick-up by the Owner on behalf of the Resident. The Parties acknowledge that no representation, inducements, promises, or agreements have been made by or on behalf of any party, except those covenants and agreements in this written agreement. Where context requires, the singular will include the plural, the plural the singular, and genders will include all genders. All Federal, State, and local laws apply where omitted.

Owner **STRONGLY** recommends that Resident **NOT** make arrangements to have packages delivered to the Premises unless Resident is available to receive them. However, if packages are received by the Owner, Resident agrees to the following:

1. Resident understands Owner picking-up packages is a convenience to the Resident and Resident agrees not to hold Owner responsible for damage, loss, or theft.

2. Resident understands Owner will **NOT** accept packages larger than 12"x12"x12" or 30+ lbs.

3. Packages may be picked-up at _____
   _____during normal business hours.

4. Resident understands Owner does not promise, warrant, or guarantee the safety or security of Resident's packages against criminal actions. Residents are responsibility for insurance.

Comments: _____
_____
_____
_____

By signing below, Resident confirms that he/she has received, reviewed, and understands this Addendum.

_____	_____	_____	_____
Resident/Lessee	Date	Resident/Lessee	Date
_____	_____	_____	_____
Resident/Lessee	Date	Resident/Lessee	Date
_____	_____	_____	_____
Owner/Lessor or Owner Agent/ Lessor Agent	Date	Owner/Lessor or Owner Agent/ Lessor Agent	Date

Smoke Detector Addendum to Lease Agreement

This Addendum is entered into by and between _____,

"Owner/Agent" and _____, "Resident."

Resident is renting from Owner the "Premises" located at: _____

_____

This Addendum is incorporated into the Lease Agreement between Lessor and Lessee, and this Addendum controls in the event of conflict with the Lease Agreement. The term of this Addendum will begin on the commencement date set forth in this Addendum and end on the expiration date set forth in the Lease Agreement unless otherwise provided in this Addendum or subsequent writing(s). This Addendum supersedes all oral and prior written agreements regarding smoke detectors. The Parties acknowledge that no representation, inducements, promises, or agreements have been made by or on behalf of any party, except those covenants and agreements in this written agreement. Where context requires, the singular will include the plural, the plural the singular, and genders all genders. All Federal, State, and local laws apply where omitted. In consideration of the mutual promises, Owner and Resident agree:

1. Resident acknowledges that Owner has installed functioning smoke detectors devices that were tested by the Owner, are operational at the time of move-in, and are operating properly.

2. Resident acknowledges that Resident is prohibited from disabling the smoke detectors.

3. Resident acknowledges that Resident is required to test smoke detectors monthly (or as recommended by the manufacturer) and replace batteries as needed.

4. Resident is required to promptly report in writing any smoke detector malfunction.

5. In accordance with State and local laws, Resident must allow Owner to access the Premises to verify that all of the smoke detectors are operating properly and to conduct maintenance services, repairs, and replacements as needed on the smoke detectors.

6. Resident will be charged for any missing or broken smoke detectors.

7. Resident acknowledge that Owner will not be liable for damages or injuries to persons or property caused by Resident or third parties disabling of smoke detectors or failure to regularly test smoke detectors, change batteries, or immediately report malfunctions to Owner.

Comments: _____

By signing below, Resident confirms that he/she has received, reviewed, and understands this Addendum.

_____	_____	_____	_____
Resident/Lessee	Date	Resident/Lessee	Date
_____	_____	_____	_____
Resident/Lessee	Date	Resident/Lessee	Date
_____	_____	_____	_____
Owner/Lessor or Owner Agent/ Lessor Agent	Date	Owner/Lessor or Owner Agent/ Lessor Agent	Date

Carbon Monoxide Detector Addendum to Lease Agreement

This Addendum is entered into by and between _____ ,

"Owner/Agent" and _____ , "Resident."

Resident is renting from Owner the "Premises" located at: _____

_____

This Addendum is incorporated into the Lease Agreement between Lessor and Lessee with this Addendum controlling in the event of conflict. The term of this Addendum will begin on the commencement date set forth in this Addendum and end on the expiration date set forth in the Lease Agreement unless otherwise provided in this Addendum or subsequent writing(s). This Addendum supersedes all oral and prior written agreements regarding detectors. The Parties acknowledge that no representation, inducements, promises, or agreements have been made by or on behalf of any party, except those covenants and agreements in this written agreement. Where context requires, the singular will include the plural, the plural the singular, and gender all genders. All Federal, State, and local laws apply where omitted. In consideration of mutual promises, Owner and Resident agree:

1. Resident acknowledges that Owner has installed functioning carbon monoxide detector that was tested by the Owner, operational at the time of move-in, and operating properly.

2. Resident acknowledges that Resident is prohibited from disabling the carbon monoxide detector.

3. Resident acknowledges that Resident is required to test the carbon monoxide detector monthly (or as recommended by the manufacturer) and replace batteries as needed.

4. Resident is required to promptly report in writing any carbon monoxide detector malfunction.

5. In accordance with State and local law, Resident must allow Owner to access the Premises to verify that the carbon monoxide detector is operating properly and to conduct maintenance services, repairs, and replacements as needed on the carbon monoxide detector.

6. Resident will be charged for any missing or broken carbon monoxide detector detectors.

7. Resident acknowledge that Owner will not be liable for damages or injuries to persons or property caused by Resident or third parties disabling of carbon monoxide detector or failure to regularly test detectors, change batteries, or immediately report malfunctions to Owner.

Comments: _____

By signing below, Resident confirms that he/she has received, reviewed, and understands this Addendum.

_____	_____	_____	_____
Resident/Lessee	Date	Resident/Lessee	Date

_____	_____	_____	_____
Resident/Lessee	Date	Resident/Lessee	Date

_____	_____	_____	_____
Owner/Lessor or Owner Agent/ Lessor Agent	Date	Owner/Lessor or Owner Agent/ Lessor Agent	Date

73

Asbestos Notification Addendum to Lease Agreement

⚠ **WARNING**

This Addendum is entered into by and between _____,

"Owner/Agent" and _____, "Resident."

Resident is renting from Owner the "Premises" located at: _____

_____

This Addendum is incorporated into the Lease Agreement between Lessor and Lessee, and this Addendum controls in the event of conflict with the Lease Agreement. The term of this Addendum will begin on the commencement date set forth in this Addendum and end on the expiration date set forth in the Lease Agreement unless otherwise provided in this Addendum or subsequent writing(s). This Addendum supersedes all oral and prior written agreements regarding asbestos. The Parties acknowledge that no representation, inducements, promises, or agreements have been made by or on behalf of any party, except those covenants and agreements in this written agreement. Where context requires, the singular will include the plural, the plural the singular, and genders will include all genders. All Federal, State, and local laws apply where omitted. In consideration of the mutual promises, Owner and Resident agree as follows:

Asbestos is a building material commonly found in buildings constructed before 1981. It has been determined that the mere existence of Asbestos does not pose a health risk as long as the asbestos is not disturbed and the fibers are not released into the air. As such, owners and residents must take reasonable precautions to minimize the risk of disturbance of asbestos materials.

This Addendum is intended as a WARNING that the Premises may contain asbestos, which may be present in buildings constructed prior to 1981 and may expose him/her to a chemical known to cause cancer.

The terms of this Addendum are intended by the Parties to be added to, and incorporated, into the Lease Agreement that currently governs the tenancy.

(Owner/Agent must check one)

❑ Owner/Agent discloses that the Premises contains asbestos materials and/or asbestos hazards that are located in or around the following areas of the Premises: _____

_____

_____

_____

_____

_____

_____

❑ Owner/Agent has no knowledge of asbestos containing materials and/or asbestos hazards located in or around the Premises; however, Owner/Agent notifies Resident that the Premises may contain asbestos materials.

❑ Owner/Agent has no knowledge of asbestos and/or asbestos hazards located in or around the Premises.

Resident understands and agrees that he/she must take reasonable steps to minimize the risk of exposure to asbestos-materials, and he/she will not do anything that may disturb the building materials of the Premises in a manner that may cause the asbestos fibers to be released. This includes, but is not limited to the following:

1. Scraping, pounding, sanding or remodeling any portion of the Premises that may release dust may cause asbestos-material to be released into the air;

2. Making repairs, improvements, or alterations to the Premises without obtaining Owner/ Agent's prior written consent and (when appropriate) providing Owner/Agent with a plan to prevent the release or exposure of any asbestos; and

3. Limiting contact with the ceiling of the Premises, including not doing the following to the ceiling: hanging hooks or other objects, penetrating the ceiling, drilling holes or attaching fixtures, allowing objects to come in contact with the ceiling, limiting water contact, cleaning or painting the ceiling, repairing or installing light fixtures, and other activities that may cause damage or disturbance to the ceiling or other asbestos-material located within the Premises.

Resident agrees to immediately notify Owner/Agent in writing of any signs of asbestos disturbance or other damage to the Premises, such as crumbling, cracking, peeling or deterioration of the walls or ceiling. Resident also agrees to immediately notify Owner/Agent in writing if any of the above stated activities in paragraphs 1-3 occur. For more information on asbestos, visit the Environmental Protection Agencies website at: http://www.epa.gov/iaq/asbestos.html or contact them by calling (202) 554-1404.

Comments: _____

_____

_____

_____

_____

By signing below, Resident confirms that he/she has received, reviewed, and understands this Addendum.

_____	_____	_____	_____
Resident/Lessee	Date	Resident/Lessee	Date
_____	_____	_____	_____
Resident/Lessee	Date	Resident/Lessee	Date
_____	_____	_____	_____
Owner/Lessor or Owner Agent/ Lessor Agent	Date	Owner/Lessor or Owner Agent/ Lessor Agent	Date

Proposition 65 Addendum to Lease Agreement (California)

⚠ WARNING

This Addendum is entered into by and between _____,

"Owner/Agent" and _____, "Resident."

Resident is renting from Owner the "Premises" located at: _____

_____

This Addendum is incorporated into the Lease Agreement between Lessor and Lessee, and this Addendum controls in the event of conflict with the Lease Agreement. The term of this Addendum will begin on the commencement date set forth in this Addendum and end on the expiration date set forth in the Lease Agreement unless otherwise provided in this Addendum or subsequent writing(s). This Addendum supersedes all oral and prior written agreements regarding asbestos. The Parties acknowledge that no representation, inducements, promises, or agreements have been made by or on behalf of any party, except those covenants and agreements in this written agreement. Where context requires, the singular will include the plural, the plural the singular, and genders will include all genders. All Federal, State, and local laws apply where omitted. In consideration of the mutual promises, Owner and Resident agree as follows:

Asbestos is a building material commonly found in buildings constructed before 1981. It has been determined that the mere existence of Asbestos does not pose a health risk as long as the asbestos is not disturbed and the fibers are not released into the air. As such, owners and residents must take reasonable precautions to minimize the risk of disturbance of asbestos materials.

This Addendum is intended as a WARNING that the Premises may contain asbestos, which may be present in buildings constructed prior to 1981 and may expose him/her to a chemical known to cause cancer.

The terms of this Addendum are intended by the Parties to be added to, and incorporated, into the Lease Agreement that currently governs the tenancy.

(Owner/Agent must check one)

- ❑ Owner/Agent discloses that the Premises contains asbestos materials and/or asbestos hazards that are located in or around the following areas of the Premises: _____

_____

_____

_____

_____

_____

_____

❑ Owner/Agent has no knowledge of asbestos containing materials and/or asbestos hazards located in or around the Premises; however, Owner/Agent notifies Resident that the Premises may contain asbestos materials.

❑ Owner/Agent has no knowledge of asbestos and/or asbestos hazards located in or around the Premises.

Resident understands and agrees that he/she must take reasonable steps to minimize the risk of exposure to asbestos-materials, and he/she will not do anything that may disturb the building materials of the Premises in a manner that may cause the asbestos fibers to be released. This includes, but is not limited to the following:

1. Scraping, pounding, sanding or remodeling any portion of the Premises that may release dust may cause asbestos-material to be released into the air;

2. Making repairs, improvements, or alterations to the Premises without obtaining Owner/ Agent's prior written consent and (when appropriate) providing Owner/Agent with a plan to prevent the release or exposure of any asbestos; and

3. Limiting contact with the ceiling of the Premises, including not doing the following to the ceiling: hanging hooks or other objects, penetrating the ceiling, drilling holes or attaching fixtures, allowing objects to come in contact with the ceiling, limiting water contact, cleaning or painting the ceiling, repairing or installing light fixtures, and other activities that may cause damage or disturbance to the ceiling or other asbestos-material located within the Premises.

Resident agrees to immediately notify Owner/Agent in writing of any signs of asbestos disturbance or other damage to the Premises, such as crumbling, cracking, peeling or deterioration of the walls or ceiling. Resident also agrees to immediately notify Owner/Agent in writing if any of the above stated activities in paragraphs 1-3 occur. For more information on asbestos, visit www.P65Warnings.ca.gov/Premises/.

Comments: _____

_____

_____

_____

_____

_____

By signing below, Resident confirms that he/she has received, reviewed, and understands this Addendum.

_____	_____	_____	_____
Resident/Lessee	Date	Resident/Lessee	Date
_____	_____	_____	_____
Resident/Lessee	Date	Resident/Lessee	Date
_____	_____	_____	_____
Owner/Lessor or Owner Agent/ Lessor Agent	Date	Owner/Lessor or Owner Agent/ Lessor Agent	Date

Disclosure of Information on Lead-Based Paint and/or Lead-Based Paint Hazards

Lead Warning Statement

Housing built before 1978 may contain lead-based paint. Lead from paint, paint chips, and dust can pose health hazards if not managed properly. Lead exposure is especially harmful to young children and pregnant women. Before renting pre-1978 housing, lessors must disclose the presence of known lead-based paint and/or lead-based paint hazards in the dwelling. Lessees must also receive a federally approved pamphlet on lead poisoning prevention.

Lessor's Disclosure

a) Presence of lead-based paint and/or lead-based paint hazards (check (i) or (ii) below):

❑ (i) Known lead-based paint and/or lead-based paint hazards are present in the housing (explain).

_____

_____

❑ (ii) Lessor has no knowledge of lead-based paint and/or lead-based paint hazards in the housing.

b) Records and reports available to the lessor (check (i) or (ii) below):

❑ (i) Lessor has provided the lessee with all available records and reports pertaining to lead-based paint and/or lead-based paint hazards in the housing (list documents below).

_____

_____

❑ (ii) Lessor has no reports or records pertaining to lead-based paint and/or lead-based paint hazards in the housing.

Lessee's Acknowledgment (initial)

c) _____ Lessee has received copies of all information listed above.

d) _____ Lessee has received the pamphlet *Protect Your Family from Lead in Your Home*.

Agent's Acknowledgment (initial)

e) _____ Agent has informed the lessor of the lessor's obligations under 42 U.S.C. 4852d and is aware of his/her responsibility to ensure compliance.

Certification of Accuracy

The following parties have reviewed the information above and certify, to the best of their knowledge, that the information they have provided is true and accurate.

Lessor/Owner	Date	Lessor/Owner	Date
Lessee/Resident	Date	Lessee/Resident	Date
Lessor Agent/Owner Agent	Date	Lessor Agent/Owner Agent	Date

Protect Your Family From Lead in Your Home

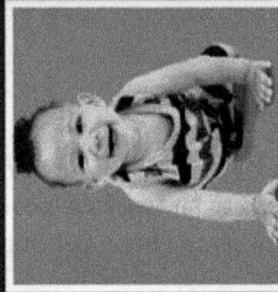

&EPA United States
Environmental
Protection Agency

United States
Consumer Product
Safety Commission

United States
Department of Housing
and Urban Development

June 2017

IMPORTANT!

Lead From Paint, Dust, and Soil in and Around Your Home Can Be Dangerous if Not Managed Properly

- Children under 6 years old are most at risk for lead poisoning in your home.

- Lead exposure can harm young children and babies even before they are born.

- Homes, schools, and child care facilities built before 1978 are likely to contain lead-based paint.

- Even children who seem healthy may have dangerous levels of lead in their bodies.

- Disturbing surfaces with lead-based paint or removing lead-based paint improperly can increase the danger to your family.

- People can get lead into their bodies by breathing or swallowing lead dust, or by eating soil or paint chips containing lead.

- People have many options for reducing lead hazards. Generally, lead-based paint that is in good condition is not a hazard (see page 10).

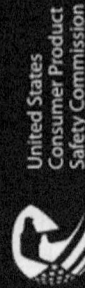

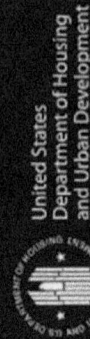

Consumer Product Safety Commission (CPSC)

The CPSC protects the public against unreasonable risk of injury from consumer products through education, safety standards activities, and enforcement. Contact CPSC for further information regarding consumer product safety and regulations.

CPSC
4330 East West Highway
Bethesda, MD 20814-4421
1-800-638-2772
cpsc.gov or saferproducts.gov

U. S. Department of Housing and Urban Development (HUD)

HUD's mission is to create strong, sustainable, inclusive communities and quality affordable homes for all. Contact HUD's Office of Healthy Homes and Lead Hazard Control for further information regarding the Lead Safe Housing Rule, which protects families in pre-1978 assisted housing, and for the lead hazard control and research grant programs.

HUD
451 Seventh Street, SW, Room 8236
Washington, DC 20410-3000
(202) 402-7698
hud.gov/offices/lead/

This document is in the public domain. It may be produced by an individual or organization without permission. Information provided in this booklet is based upon current scientific and technical understanding of the issues presented and is reflective of the jurisdictional boundaries established by the statutes governing the co-authoring agencies. Following the advice given will not necessarily provide complete protection in all situations or against all health hazards that can be caused by lead exposure.

U.S. EPA Washington DC 20460
U.S. CPSC Bethesda MD 20814
U.S. HUD Washington DC 20410

EPA-747-K-12-001
June 2017

Are You Planning to Buy or Rent a Home Built Before 1978?

Did you know that many homes built before 1978 have **lead-based paint**? Lead from paint, chips, and dust can pose serious health hazards.

Read this entire brochure to learn:

- How lead gets into the body
- How lead affects health
- What you can do to protect your family
- Where to go for more information

Before renting or buying a pre-1978 home or apartment, federal law requires:

- Sellers must disclose known information on lead-based paint or lead-based paint hazards before selling a house.
- Real estate sales contracts must include a specific warning statement about lead-based paint. Buyers have up to 10 days to check for lead.
- Landlords must disclose known information on lead-based paint and lead-based paint hazards before leases take effect. Leases must include a specific warning statement about lead-based paint.

If undertaking renovations, repairs, or painting (RRP) projects in your pre-1978 home or apartment:

- Read EPA's pamphlet, *The Lead-Safe Certified Guide to Renovate Right*, to learn about the lead-safe work practices that contractors are required to follow when working in your home (see page 12).

Simple Steps to Protect Your Family from Lead Hazards

If you think your home has lead-based paint:

- Don't try to remove lead-based paint yourself.

- Always keep painted surfaces in good condition to minimize deterioration.

- Get your home checked for lead hazards. Find a certified inspector or risk assessor at epa.gov/lead.

- Talk to your landlord about fixing surfaces with peeling or chipping paint.

- Regularly clean floors, window sills, and other surfaces.

- Take precautions to avoid exposure to lead dust when remodeling.

- When renovating, repairing, or painting, hire only EPA- or state-approved Lead-Safe certified renovation firms.

- Before buying, renting, or renovating your home, have it checked for lead-based paint.

- Consult your health care provider about testing your children for lead. Your pediatrician can check for lead with a simple blood test.

- Wash children's hands, bottles, pacifiers, and toys often.

- Make sure children eat healthy, low-fat foods high in iron, calcium, and vitamin C.

- Remove shoes or wipe soil off shoes before entering your house.

U. S. Environmental Protection Agency (EPA) Regional Offices

The mission of EPA is to protect human health and the environment. Your Regional EPA Office can provide further information regarding regulations and lead protection programs.

Region 1 (Connecticut, Massachusetts, Maine, New Hampshire, Rhode Island, Vermont)

Regional Lead Contact
U.S. EPA Region 1
5 Post Office Square, Suite 100, OES 05-4
Boston, MA 02109-3912
(888) 372-7341

Region 2 (New Jersey, New York, Puerto Rico, Virgin Islands)

Regional Lead Contact
U.S. EPA Region 2
2890 Woodbridge Avenue
Building 205, Mail Stop 225
Edison, NJ 08837-3679
(732) 321-6671

Region 3 (Delaware, Maryland, Pennsylvania, Virginia, DC, West Virginia)

Regional Lead Contact
U.S. EPA Region 3
1650 Arch Street
Philadelphia, PA 19103
(215) 814-2088

Region 4 (Alabama, Florida, Georgia, Kentucky, Mississippi, North Carolina, South Carolina, Tennessee)

Regional Lead Contact
U.S. EPA Region 4
AFC Tower, 12th Floor, Air, Pesticides & Toxics
61 Forsyth Street, SW
Atlanta, GA 30303
(404) 562-8998

Region 5 (Illinois, Indiana, Michigan, Minnesota, Ohio, Wisconsin)

Regional Lead Contact
U.S. EPA Region 5 (DT-8J)
77 West Jackson Boulevard
Chicago, IL 60604-3666
(312) 886-7836

Region 6 (Arkansas, Louisiana, New Mexico, Oklahoma, Texas, and 66 Tribes)

Regional Lead Contact
U.S. EPA Region 6
1445 Ross Avenue, 12th Floor
Dallas, TX 75202-2733
(214) 665-2704

Region 7 (Iowa, Kansas, Missouri, Nebraska)

Regional Lead Contact
U.S. EPA Region 7
11201 Renner Blvd.
WWPD/TOPE
Lenexa, KS 66219
(800) 223-0425

Region 8 (Colorado, Montana, North Dakota, South Dakota, Utah, Wyoming)

Regional Lead Contact
U.S. EPA Region 8
1595 Wynkoop St.
Denver, CO 80202
(303) 312-6966

Region 9 (Arizona, California, Hawaii, Nevada)

Regional Lead Contact
U.S. EPA Region 9 (CMD-4-2)
75 Hawthorne Street
San Francisco, CA 94105
(415) 947-4280

Region 10 (Alaska, Idaho, Oregon, Washington)

Regional Lead Contact
U.S. EPA Region 10
Solid Waste & Toxics Unit (WCM-128)
1200 Sixth Avenue, Suite 900
Seattle, WA 98101
(206) 553-1200

Lead Gets into the Body in Many Ways

Adults and children can get lead into their bodies if they:

- Breathe in lead dust (especially during activities such as renovations, repairs, or painting that disturb painted surfaces).

- Swallow lead dust that has settled on food, food preparation surfaces, and other places.

- Eat paint chips or soil that contains lead.

Lead is especially dangerous to children under the age of 6.

- At this age, children's brains and nervous systems are more sensitive to the damaging effects of lead.

- Children's growing bodies absorb more lead.

- Babies and young children often put their hands and other objects in their mouths. These objects can have lead dust on them.

Women of childbearing age should know that lead is dangerous to a developing fetus.

- Women with a high lead level in their system before or during pregnancy risk exposing the fetus to lead through the placenta during fetal development.

For More Information

The National Lead Information Center
Learn how to protect children from lead poisoning and get other information about lead hazards on the Web at epa.gov/lead and hud.gov/lead, or call **1-800-424-LEAD (5323)**.

EPA's Safe Drinking Water Hotline
For information about lead in drinking water, call **1-800-426-4791**, or visit epa.gov/safewater for information about lead in drinking water.

Consumer Product Safety Commission (CPSC) Hotline
For information on lead in toys and other consumer products, or to report an unsafe consumer product or a product-related injury, call **1-800-638-2772**, or visit CPSC's website at cpsc.gov or saferproducts.gov.

State and Local Health and Environmental Agencies
Some states, tribes, and cities have their own rules related to lead-based paint. Check with your local agency to see which laws apply to you. Most agencies can also provide information on finding a lead abatement firm in your area, and on possible sources of financial aid for reducing lead hazards. Receive up-to-date address and phone information for your state or local contacts on the Web at epa.gov/lead, or contact the National Lead Information Center at **1-800-424-LEAD.**

Hearing- or speech-challenged individuals may access any of the phone numbers in this brochure through TTY by calling the toll-free Federal Relay Service at **1-800-877-8339**.

Other Sources of Lead, continued

- **Lead smelters** or other industries that release lead into the air.

- **Your job.** If you work with lead, you could bring it home on your body or clothes. Shower and change clothes before coming home. Launder your work clothes separately from the rest of your family's clothes.

- **Hobbies** that use lead, such as making pottery or stained glass, or refinishing furniture. Call your local health department for information about hobbies that may use lead.

- Old **toys** and **furniture** may have been painted with lead-containing paint. Older toys and other children's products may have parts that contain lead.[4]

- Food and liquids cooked or stored in **lead crystal** or **lead-glazed pottery or porcelain** may contain lead.

- Folk remedies, such as **"greta"** and **"azarcon,"** used to treat an upset stomach.

---

[4] In 1978, the federal government banned toys, other children's products, and furniture with lead-containing paint. In 2008, the federal government banned lead in most children's products. The federal government currently bans lead in excess of 100 ppm by weight in most children's products.

Health Effects of Lead

Lead affects the body in many ways. It is important to know that even exposure to low levels of lead can severely harm children.

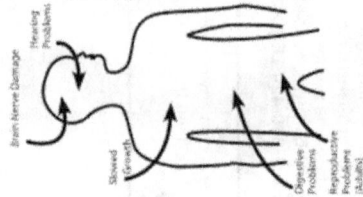

In children, exposure to lead can cause:

- Nervous system and kidney damage
- Learning disabilities, attention-deficit disorder, and decreased intelligence
- Speech, language, and behavior problems
- Poor muscle coordination
- Decreased muscle and bone growth
- Hearing damage

While low-lead exposure is most common, exposure to high amounts of lead can have devastating effects on children, including seizures, unconsciousness, and in some cases, death.

Although children are especially susceptible to lead exposure, lead can be dangerous for adults, too.

In adults, exposure to lead can cause:

- Harm to a developing fetus
- Increased chance of high blood pressure during pregnancy
- Fertility problems (in men and women)
- High blood pressure
- Digestive problems
- Nerve disorders
- Memory and concentration problems
- Muscle and joint pain

Check Your Family for Lead

Get your children and home tested if you think your home has lead.

Children's blood lead levels tend to increase rapidly from 6 to 12 months of age, and tend to peak at 18 to 24 months of age.

Consult your doctor for advice on testing your children. A simple blood test can detect lead. Blood lead tests are usually recommended for:

- Children at ages 1 and 2
- Children or other family members who have been exposed to high levels of lead
- Children who should be tested under your state or local health screening plan

Your doctor can explain what the test results mean and if more testing will be needed.

Other Sources of Lead

Lead in Drinking Water

The most common sources of lead in drinking water are lead pipes, faucets, and fixtures.

Lead pipes are more likely to be found in older cities and homes built before 1986.

You can't smell or taste lead in drinking water.

To find out for certain if you have lead in drinking water, have your water tested.

Remember older homes with a private well can also have plumbing materials that contain lead.

Important Steps You Can Take to Reduce Lead in Drinking Water

- Use only cold water for drinking, cooking and making baby formula. Remember, boiling water does not remove lead from water.
- Before drinking, flush your home's pipes by running the tap, taking a shower, doing laundry, or doing a load of dishes.
- Regularly clean your faucet's screen (also known as an aerator).
- If you use a filter certified to remove lead, don't forget to read the directions to learn when to change the cartridge. Using a filter after it has expired can make it less effective at removing lead.

Contact your water company to determine if the pipe that connects your home to the water main (called a service line) is made from lead. Your area's water company can also provide information about the lead levels in your system's drinking water.

For more information about lead in drinking water, please contact EPA's Safe Drinking Water Hotline at 1-800-426-4791. If you have other questions about lead poisoning prevention, call 1-800 424-LEAD.*

Call your local health department or water company to find out about testing your water, or visit epa.gov/safewater for EPA's lead in drinking water information. Some states or utilities offer programs to pay for water testing for residents. Contact your state or local water company to learn more.

---

* Hearing- or speech-challenged individuals may access this number through TTY by calling the Federal Relay Service at 1-800-877-8339.

Renovating, Repairing or Painting a Home with Lead-Based Paint

If you hire a contractor to conduct renovation, repair, or painting (RRP) projects in your pre-1978 home or childcare facility (such as pre-school and kindergarten), your contractor must:

- Be a Lead-Safe Certified firm approved by EPA or an EPA-authorized state program

- Use qualified trained individuals (Lead-Safe Certified renovators) who follow specific lead-safe work practices to prevent lead contamination

- Provide a copy of EPA's lead hazard information document, *The Lead-Safe Certified Guide to Renovate Right*

RRP contractors working in pre-1978 homes and childcare facilities must follow lead-safe work practices that:

- **Contain the work area.** The area must be contained so that dust and debris do not escape from the work area. Warning signs must be put up, and plastic or other impermeable material and tape must be used.

- **Avoid renovation methods that generate large amounts of lead-contaminated dust.** Some methods generate so much lead-contaminated dust that their use is prohibited. They are:

  - Open-flame burning or torching

  - Sanding, grinding, planing, needle gunning, or blasting with power tools and equipment not equipped with a shroud and HEPA vacuum attachment

  - Using a heat gun at temperatures greater than 1100°F

- **Clean up thoroughly.** The work area should be cleaned up daily. When all the work is done, the area must be cleaned up using special cleaning methods.

- **Dispose of waste properly.** Collect and seal waste in a heavy duty bag or sheeting. When transported, ensure that waste is contained to prevent release of dust and debris.

To learn more about EPA's requirements for RRP projects, visit epa.gov/getleadsafe, or read *The Lead-Safe Certified Guide to Renovate Right*.

12

Where Lead-Based Paint Is Found

In general, the older your home or childcare facility, the more likely it has lead-based paint.[1]

Many homes, including private, federally-assisted, federally-owned housing, and childcare facilities built before 1978 have lead-based paint. In 1978, the federal government banned consumer uses of lead-containing paint.[2]

Learn how to determine if paint is lead-based paint on page 7.

Lead can be found:

- In homes and childcare facilities in the city, country, or suburbs,

- In private and public single-family homes and apartments,

- On surfaces inside and outside of the house, and

- In soil around a home. (Soil can pick up lead from exterior paint or other sources, such as past use of leaded gas in cars.)

Learn more about where lead is found at epa.gov/lead.

---

[1] "Lead-based paint" is currently defined by the federal government as paint with lead levels greater than or equal to 1.0 milligram per square centimeter (mg/cm), or more than 0.5% by weight.

[2] "Lead-containing paint" is currently defined by the federal government as lead in new dried paint in excess of 90 parts per million (ppm) by weight.

Reducing Lead Hazards, continued

If your home has had lead abatement work done or if the housing is receiving federal assistance, once the work is completed, dust cleanup activities must be conducted until clearance testing indicates that lead dust levels are below the following levels:

- 40 micrograms per square foot ($\mu g/ft^2$) for floors, including carpeted floors
- 250 $\mu g/ft^2$ for interior windows sills
- 400 $\mu g/ft^2$ for window troughs

For help in locating certified lead abatement professionals in your area, call your state or local agency (see pages 14 and 15), or visit epa.gov/lead, or call 1-800-424-LEAD.

Identifying Lead-Based Paint and Lead-Based Paint Hazards

Deteriorating lead-based paint (peeling, chipping, chalking, cracking, or damaged paint) is a hazard and needs immediate attention. **Lead-based paint** may also be a hazard when found on surfaces that children can chew or that get a lot of wear and tear, such as:

- On windows and window sills
- Doors and door frames
- Stairs, railings, banisters, and porches

Lead-based paint is usually not a hazard if it is in good condition and if it is not on an impact or friction surface like a window.

Lead dust can form when lead-based paint is scraped, sanded, or heated. Lead dust also forms when painted surfaces containing lead bump or rub together. Lead paint chips and dust can get on surfaces and objects that people touch. Settled lead dust can reenter the air when the home is vacuumed or swept, or when people walk through it. EPA currently defines the following levels of lead in dust as hazardous:

- 40 micrograms per square foot ($\mu g/ft^2$) and higher for floors, including carpeted floors
- 250 $\mu g/ft^2$ and higher for interior window sills

Lead in soil can be a hazard when children play in bare soil or when people bring soil into the house on their shoes. EPA currently defines the following levels of lead in soil as hazardous:

- 400 parts per million (ppm) and higher in play areas of bare soil
- 1,200 ppm (average) and higher in bare soil in the remainder of the yard

Remember, lead from paint chips—which you can see—and lead dust—which you may not be able to see—both can be hazards.

The only way to find out if paint, dust, or soil lead hazards exist is to test for them. The next page describes how to do this.

Checking Your Home for Lead

You can get your home tested for lead in several different ways:

- A lead-based paint **inspection** tells you if your home has lead-based paint and where it is located. It won't tell you whether your home currently has lead hazards. A trained and certified testing professional, called a lead-based paint inspector, will conduct a paint inspection using methods, such as:

  - Portable x-ray fluorescence (XRF) machine
  - Lab tests of paint samples

- A **risk assessment** tells you if your home currently has any lead hazards from lead in paint, dust, or soil. It also tells you what actions to take to address any hazards. A trained and certified testing professional, called a risk assessor, will:

  - Sample paint that is deteriorated on doors, windows, floors, stairs, and walls

  - Sample dust near painted surfaces and sample bare soil in the yard

  - Get lab tests of paint, dust, and soil samples

- A combination inspection and risk assessment tells you if your home has any lead-based paint and if your home has any lead hazards, and where both are located.

Be sure to read the report provided to you after your inspection or risk assessment is completed, and ask questions about anything you do not understand.

Reducing Lead Hazards

Disturbing lead-based paint or removing lead improperly can increase the hazard to your family by spreading even more lead dust around the house.

- In addition to day-to-day cleaning and good nutrition, you can **temporarily** reduce lead-based paint hazards by taking actions, such as repairing damaged painted surfaces and planting grass to cover lead-contaminated soil. These actions are not permanent solutions and will need ongoing attention.

- You can minimize exposure to lead when renovating, repairing, or painting by hiring an EPA- or state-certified renovator who is trained in the use of lead-safe work practices. If you are a do-it-yourselfer, learn how to use lead-safe work practices in your home.

- To remove lead hazards permanently, you should hire a certified lead abatement contractor. Abatement (or permanent hazard elimination) methods include removing, sealing, or enclosing lead-based paint with special materials. Just painting over the hazard with regular paint is not permanent control.

Always use a certified contractor who is trained to address lead hazards safely.

- Hire a Lead-Safe Certified firm (see page 12) to perform renovation, repair, or painting (RRP) projects that disturb painted surfaces.

- To correct lead hazards permanently, hire a certified lead abatement professional. This will ensure your contractor knows how to work safely and has the proper equipment to clean up thoroughly.

Certified contractors will employ qualified workers and follow strict safety rules as set by their state or by the federal government.

Checking Your Home for Lead, continued

In preparing for renovation, repair, or painting work in a pre-1978 home, Lead-Safe Certified renovators (see page 12) may:

- Take paint chip samples to determine if lead-based paint is present in the area planned for renovation and send them to an EPA-recognized lead lab for analysis. In housing receiving federal assistance, the person collecting these samples must be a certified lead-based paint inspector or risk assessor

- Use EPA-recognized tests kits to determine if lead-based paint is absent (but not in housing receiving federal assistance)

- Presume that lead-based paint is present and use lead-safe work practices

There are state and federal programs in place to ensure that testing is done safely, reliably, and effectively. Contact your state or local agency for more information, visit epa.gov/lead, or call **1-800-424-LEAD (5323)** for a list of contacts in your area.[3]

What You Can Do Now to Protect Your Family

If you suspect that your house has lead-based paint hazards, you can take some immediate steps to reduce your family's risk:

- If you rent, notify your landlord of peeling or chipping paint.

- Keep painted surfaces clean and free of dust. Clean floors, window frames, window sills, and other surfaces weekly. Use a mop or sponge with warm water and a general all-purpose cleaner. (Remember: never mix ammonia and bleach products together because they can form a dangerous gas.)

- Carefully clean up paint chips immediately without creating dust.

- Thoroughly rinse sponges and mop heads often during cleaning of dirty or dusty areas, and again afterward.

- Wash your hands and your children's hands often, especially before they eat and before nap time and bed time.

- Keep play areas clean. Wash bottles, pacifiers, toys, and stuffed animals regularly.

- Keep children from chewing window sills or other painted surfaces, or eating soil.

- When renovating, repairing, or painting, hire only EPA- or state-approved Lead-Safe Certified renovation firms (see page 12).

- Clean or remove shoes before entering your home to avoid tracking in lead from soil.

- Make sure children eat nutritious, low-fat meals high in iron, and calcium, such as spinach and dairy products. Children with good diets absorb less lead.

[3] Hearing- or speech-challenged individuals may access this number through TTY by calling the Federal Relay Service at 1-800-877-8339.

Declaración de Información sobre Pintura a Base de Plomo y/o Peligros de la Pintura a Base de Plomo

Declaración sobre los Peligros del Plomo

Las viviendas construidas antes del año 1978 pueden contener pintura a base de plomo. El plomo de pintura, pedazos de pintura y polvo puede representar peligros para la salud si no se maneja apropiadamente. La exposición al plomo es especialmente dañino para los niños jóvenes y las mujeres embarazadas. Antes de alquilar (rentar) una vivienda construida antes del año 1978, los arrendadores tienen la obligación de informar sobre la presencia de pintura a base de plomo o peligros de pintura a base de plomo conocidos en la vivienda. Los arrendatarios (inquilinos) también deben recibir un folleto aprobado por el Gobierno Federal sobre la prevención del envenenamiento de plomo.

Declaración del Arrendador

a) Presencia de pintura a base de plomo y/o peligros de pintura a base de plomo (marque (i) ó (ii) abajo):

❑ (i) Confirmado que hay pintura a base de plomo y/o peligro de pintura a base de plomo en la vivienda (explique).

_____

_____

❑ (ii) El arrendador no tiene ningún conocimiento de que haya pintura a base de plomo y/o peligro de pintura a base de plomo en la vivienda.

b) Archivos e informes disponibles para el vendedor (marque (i) ó (ii) abajo):

❑ (i) El arrendador le ha proporcionado al comprador todos los archivos e informes disponibles relacionados con pintura a base de plomo y/o peligro de pintura a base de plomo en la vivienda (anote los documentos abajo).

_____

_____

❑ (ii) El arrendador no tiene archivos ni informes relacionados con pintura a base de plomo y/o peligro de pintura a base de plomo en la vivienda.

Acuse de Recibo del Arrendatario o Inquilino (inicial)

c) _____ El arrendatario ha recibido copias de toda la información indicada arriba.

d) _____ El arrendatario ha recibido el folleto titulado *Proteja a Su Familia del Plomo en Su Casa*.

Acuse de Recibo del Agente (inicial)

e) _____ El agente le ha informado al arrendador de las obligaciones del arrendador de acuerdo con 42 U.S.C. 4852d y está consciente de su responsabilidad de asegurar su cumplimiento.

Certificación de Exactitud

Las partes siguientes han revisado la información que aparece arriba y certifican que, según su entender, toda la información que han proporcionado es verdadera y exacta.

_____	_____	_____	_____
Arrendador	Fecha	Arrendador	Fecha
_____	_____	_____	_____
Arrendatario	Fecha	Arrendatario	Fecha
_____	_____	_____	_____
Agente	Fecha	Agente	Fecha

Proteja a su familia contra el plomo en el hogar

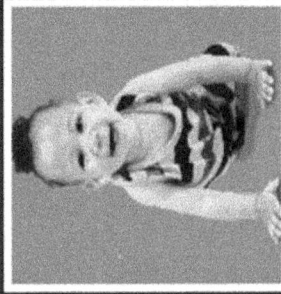

EPA — Agencia de Protección Ambiental de los Estados Unidos (EPA)

Comisión de Seguridad de Productos del Consumidor de Estados Unidos (CPSC)

Departamento de la Vivienda y de Desarrollo Urbano de los Estados Unidos (HUD)

Junio de 2017

¡IMPORTANTE!

El plomo de la pintura, del polvo y de la tierra en la casa y alrededor de esta puede ser peligroso si no se maneja adecuadamente

· Los niños menores de 6 años son los que corren mayor riesgo de envenenamiento por plomo en la casa.

· La exposición al plomo puede hacerle daño a los niños pequeños y aun a los bebés antes del nacimiento.

· Es probable que las casas, las escuelas y los centros de cuidado infantil construidos antes de 1978 contengan pintura con base de plomo.

· Aun los niños que aparentan estar saludables pueden tener niveles peligrosos de plomo en el cuerpo.

· Alterar las superficies con pintura con base de plomo o remover incorrectamente la pintura con base de plomo puede aumentar los peligros para su familia.

· El plomo puede entrar en el cuerpo de las personas al respirar o tragar polvo de plomo, o al comer tierra o partículas de pintura que contengan plomo.

· Las personas tienen muchas opciones para reducir los peligros relacionados con el plomo. Generalmente, la pintura con base de plomo que está en buenas condiciones no es peligrosa (vea la página 10).

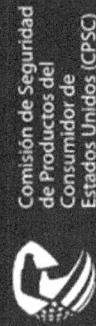

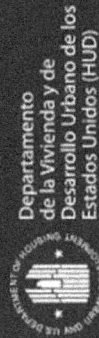

¿Está planeando comprar o alquilar una casa construida antes de 1978?

¿Sabía que muchas casas construidas antes de 1978 tienen **pintura con base de plomo**? El plomo en la pintura, las partículas y el polvo puede ser un peligro grave para la salud.

Lea todo este folleto para saber:

- Cómo entra el plomo en el cuerpo.
- Cómo el plomo afecta a la salud.
- Qué puede hacer para proteger a su familia.
- Adónde recurrir para obtener más información.

Antes de alquilar o comprar una casa o un apartamento construido antes de 1978, la ley federal requiere lo siguiente:

- Los vendedores tienen que dar la información que posean acerca de la pintura con base de plomo o los peligros relacionados con dicha pintura antes de vender una casa.
- Los contratos de venta de inmuebles deben incluir una declaración de advertencia específica sobre la pintura con base de plomo. Los compradores tienen hasta 10 días para verificar la existencia de plomo.
- Los propietarios tienen que dar la información que posean acerca de la pintura con base de plomo y los peligros relacionados con dicha pintura antes de que el alquiler entre en vigencia. Los contratos de alquiler deben incluir una declaración de advertencia específica sobre la pintura con base de plomo.

Si emprenderá algún proyecto de renovación, reparación o pintura (RRP, por sus siglas en inglés) en su casa o apartamento construido antes de 1978:

- Lea el folleto de la EPA *Guía de prácticas acreditas seguras para trabajar con el plomo para remodelar correctamente.*

Comisión de Seguridad de Productos del Consumidor de Estados Unidos (CPSC)

La CPSC protege al público contra el riesgo irrazonable de daños causados por productos del consumidor a través de educación, actividades relacionadas con normas de seguridad y aplicación de la ley. Comuníquese con la CPSC para obtener más información sobre los reglamentos y la seguridad de los productos del consumidor.

CPSC
4330 East West Highway
Bethesda, MD 20814-4421
1-800-638-2772
cpsc.gov o saferproducts.gov

Departamento de la Vivienda y de Desarrollo Urbano de los Estados Unidos (HUD)

La misión del HUD es crear comunidades fuertes, sustentables e inclusivas, así como hogares de calidad asequibles para todos. Comuníquese con la Oficina de Hogares Saludables y Control de Peligros Relacionados con el Plomo del HUD para obtener más información acerca de la Regla sobre Viviendas Seguras en relación con el Plomo, que protege a las familias que residen en viviendas construidas antes de 1978 que reciben ayuda económica, y acerca de los programas de control de los peligros relacionados con el plomo y de subvenciones para investigación.

HUD
451 Seventh Street, SW, Room 8236
Washington, DC 20410-3000
(202) 402-7698
hud.gov/offices/lead/

Este documento es del dominio público y puede ser reproducido por cualquier persona u organización sin necesidad de solicitar autorización. La información contenida en este folleto se basa en el conocimiento científico y técnico actual sobre los aspectos presentados, y refleja las barreras jurisdiccionales establecidas por los estatutos que gobiernan a las agencias que han colaborado en su preparación. Al seguir la asesoría que se ofrece, no se obtiene necesariamente una protección total para todas las situaciones o contra todos los peligros para la salud que pueden ser causa de la exposición al plomo.

U.S. EPA Washington DC 20460
U.S. CPSC Bethesda MD 20814
U.S. HUD Washington DC 20410

EPA-747-K-13-001
Junio de 2017

17

Medidas sencillas para proteger a su familia contra los peligros relacionados con el plomo

Si cree que su casa tiene pintura con base de plomo:

- No trate de remover usted mismo la pintura con base de plomo.

- Mantenga siempre las superficies pintadas en buenas condiciones para minimizar el deterioro.

- Haga que examinen su casa para identificar peligros relacionados con el plomo. Encuentre un inspector certificado o un asesor de riesgos en epa.gov/lead.

- Hable con el propietario para que arregle las superficies con pintura descascarada o picada.

- Limpie con regularidad los pisos, los antepechos de las ventanas y las demás superficies.

- Tome precauciones para evitar la exposición al polvo de plomo al remodelar.

- Al realizar renovaciones, reparaciones o pintura, contrate solamente a empresas de renovación certificadas en prácticas seguras con el plomo aprobadas por el estado o la EPA.

- Antes de comprar, alquilar o renovar su casa, hágala examinar para ver si tiene pintura con base de plomo.

- Consulte con su profesional de la salud sobre pruebas para detectar la presencia de plomo en sus hijos. El pediatra puede comprobar la presencia de plomo con un simple análisis de sangre.

- Lave con frecuencia las manos, los biberones, los chupones y los juguetes de los niños.

- Asegúrese de que los niños coman alimentos saludables, bajos en grasa, y altos en hierro, calcio y vitamina C.

- Quítese los zapatos o lave la tierra de los zapatos antes de entrar a su casa.

Oficinas regionales de la Agencia de Protección Ambiental de los Estados Unidos (EPA)

La misión de la EPA es proteger la salud de los seres humanos y el medio ambiente. La Oficina Regional de la EPA puede darle más información sobre la normativa y los programas de protección contra el plomo.

Región 1 (Connecticut, Massachusetts, Maine, New Hampshire, Rhode Island, Vermont)

Regional Lead Contact
(Contacto regional para el plomo)
U.S. EPA Region 1
Suite 1100 (CPT) One Congress Street
Boston, MA 02114-2023
(617) 918-1524

Región 2 (New Jersey, New York, Puerto Rico, Virgin Islands)

Regional Lead Contact
(Contacto regional para el plomo)
U.S. EPA Region 2
2890 Woodbridge Avenue
Building 205, Mail Stop 225
Edison NJ 08837-3679
(732) 321-6671

Región 3 (Delaware, Maryland, Pennsylvania, Virginia, DC, West Virginia)

Regional Lead Contact
(Contacto regional para el plomo)
U.S. EPA Region 3
1650 Arch Street
Philadelphia, PA 19103
(215) 814-2088

Región 4 (Alabama, Florida, Georgia, Kentucky, Mississippi, North Carolina, South Carolina, Tennessee)

Regional Lead Contact
(Contacto regional para el plomo)
U.S. EPA Region 4
AFC Tower, 12th Floor, Air, Pesticides & Toxics
61 Forsyth Street, SW
Atlanta, GA 30303
(404) 562-8998

Región 5 (Illinois, Indiana, Michigan, Minnesota, Ohio, Wisconsin)

Regional Lead Contact
(Contacto regional para el plomo)
U.S. EPA Region 5 (DT-8J)
77 West Jackson Boulevard
Chicago, IL 60604-3666
(312) 886-7836

Región 6 (Arkansas, Louisiana, New Mexico, Oklahoma, Texas y 66 tribus)

Regional Lead Contact
(Contacto regional para el plomo)
U.S. EPA Region 6
1445 Ross Avenue, 12th Floor
Dallas, TX 75202-2733
(214) 665-2704

Región 7 (Iowa, Kansas, Missouri, Nebraska)

Regional Lead Contact
(Contacto regional para el plomo)
U.S. EPA Region 7
11201 Renner Blvd.
WWPD/TOPE
Lenexa, KS 66219
(800) 223-0425

Región 8 (Colorado, Montana, North Dakota, South Dakota, Utah, Wyoming)

Regional Lead Contact
(Contacto regional para el plomo)
U.S. EPA Region 8
1595 Wynkoop St.
Denver, CO 80202
(303) 312-6966

Región 9 (Arizona, California, Hawaii, Nevada)

Regional Lead Contact
(Contacto regional para el plomo)
U.S. EPA Region 9 (CMD-4-2)
75 Hawthorne Street
San Francisco, CA 94105
(415) 947-4280

Región 10 (Alaska, Idaho, Oregon, Washington)

Regional Lead Contact
(Contacto regional para el plomo)
U.S. EPA Region 10
Solid Waste & Toxics Unit (WCM-128)
1200 Sixth Avenue, Suite 900
Seattle, WA 98101
(206) 553-1200

Para obtener más información

The National Lead Information Center (Centro Nacional de Información sobre el Plomo)

Averigüe cómo proteger a los niños del envenenamiento por plomo y obtenga otra información sobre los peligros relacionados con el plomo por Internet en epa.gov/lead y hud.gov/lead, o llame al **1-800-424-LEAD (5323)**.

Línea directa de agua potable segura de la EPA

Para obtener información sobre el plomo en el agua potable, llame al **1-800-426-4791** o visite epa.gov/lead para obtener información sobre el plomo en el agua potable.

Línea directa de la Comisión de Seguridad de Productos del Consumidor de Estados Unidos (CPSC)

Para pedir información relacionada con el plomo en los juguetes y en otros productos del consumidor, o para denunciar un producto del consumidor inseguro o una lesión relacionada con un producto, llame al **1-800-638-2772**, o visite el sitio web de la CPSC en cpsc.gov o saferproducts.gov.

Agencias del medio ambiente y de salud estatales y locales

Algunos estados, tribus y ciudades tienen sus propias reglas relacionadas con la pintura con base de plomo. Consulte con su agencia local para ver cuáles leyes se le aplican. La mayoría de las agencias también pueden proporcionarle información para encontrar en su área una empresa para remover el plomo, y para conseguir posibles fuentes de ayuda económica para la reducción de los peligros relacionados con el plomo. Obtenga direcciones e información telefónica actualizadas de contactos locales o estatales por Internet en epa.gov/lead, o comuníquese con el Centro Nacional de Información sobre el Plomo llamando al **1-800-424-LEAD**.

Las personas con impedimentos auditivos o del habla pueden acceder a cualquiera de los números de teléfono que se indican en este folleto a través del sistema TTY llamando en forma gratuita al Federal Relay Service (Servicio Federal de Retransmisión) al **1-800-877-8339**.

El plomo entra al cuerpo de muchas maneras

El plomo puede entrar en el cuerpo de adultos y niños si:

- Respiran el polvo de plomo (especialmente durante las actividades de renovación, reparación y pintura que alteran las superficies pintadas).

- Tragan polvo de plomo que se ha acumulado en alimentos, superficies donde se preparan alimentos y otros lugares.

- Comen partículas de pintura o tierra que contengan plomo.

El plomo es especialmente peligroso para los niños menores de 6 años.

- A esta edad, el cerebro y el sistema nervioso de los niños son más sensibles a los efectos dañinos del plomo.

- El cuerpo en crecimiento de los niños absorbe más plomo.

- Los bebés y los niños pequeños se llevan las manos y otros objetos a la boca con frecuencia. Dichos objetos pueden estar cubiertos de polvo de plomo.

Las mujeres en edad de concebir deben saber que el plomo es peligroso para el feto en desarrollo.

- Las mujeres que tienen un nivel alto de plomo en su cuerpo antes del embarazo o mientras están embarazadas podrían exponer al feto al plomo a través de la placenta durante su desarrollo.

Otras fuentes de plomo (continuación)

- Los **hornos de fundición de plomo** u otras industrias que emiten plomo al aire.

- **Su trabajo.** Si trabaja con plomo, podría traerlo a su casa en el cuerpo o la ropa. Báñese y cámbiese la ropa antes de volver a su casa. Lave la ropa de trabajo por separado del resto de la ropa de la familia.

- Los **pasatiempos** que usan plomo, tales como hacer trabajos en cerámica, pintar en vidrio o restaurar muebles. Llame al departamento de salud local para obtener información sobre los pasatiempos en los que puede usarse plomo.

- Los **juguetes** y **muebles** viejos que pueden haberse pintado con pintura que contenga plomo. Los juguetes viejos y otros productos para niños pueden contener partes con plomo.[4]

- Los alimentos y líquidos cocinados o almacenados en **cristal de plomo**, o en **cerámica o porcelana con esmalte de plomo** pueden contener plomo.

- Los remedios caseros, tales como **"greta"** y **"azarcón"**, que se usan para tratar padecimientos estomacales.

---

[4] En 1978, el gobierno federal prohibió los juguetes, otros productos para niños y los muebles con pintura que contenga plomo. En 2008, el gobierno federal también prohibió el plomo en la mayoría de los productos para niños, y actualmente prohíbe el plomo en cantidades superiores a 100 ppm por peso en la mayoría de los productos para niños.

14

Efectos del plomo en la salud

El plomo afecta el cuerpo de muchas maneras. Es importante saber que aun una exposición a niveles bajos de plomo puede afectar al niño gravemente.

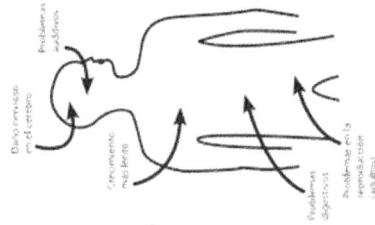

En los niños, la exposición al plomo puede causar:

- Daño al sistema nervioso y los riñones.

- Problemas de aprendizaje, desorden de deficiencia de atención y disminución de la capacidad intelectual.

- Problemas del habla, del lenguaje y de comportamiento.

- Pobre coordinación muscular.

- Disminución en el crecimiento muscular y de los huesos.

- Daño en la audición.

Mientras que la exposición a niveles bajos de plomo es más común, la exposición a niveles altos de plomo puede causar efectos devastadores en los niños, incluso convulsiones, pérdida del conocimiento y, en algunos casos, la muerte.

Aunque los niños son especialmente susceptibles a la exposición al plomo, también puede ser peligroso para los adultos.

En los adultos, la exposición al plomo puede causar:

- Daño a un feto en desarrollo.

- Mayor probabilidad de tener tensión arterial alta durante el embarazo.

- Problemas de fertilidad (en hombres y mujeres).

- Tensión arterial alta.

- Problemas digestivos.

- Trastornos nerviosos.

- Problemas de memoria y concentración.

- Dolores musculares y articulares.

3

94

Verifique el nivel de plomo en su familia

Haga que examinen a sus niños y a su casa si cree que esta tiene plomo.

El nivel de plomo en la sangre de los niños tiende a aumentar con rapidez entre los 6 y 12 meses de edad, y tiende a llegar al nivel más alto entre los 18 y 24 meses de edad.

Consulte a su médico en cuanto a la necesidad de examinar a sus niños. Un sencillo análisis de sangre puede detectar la presencia de plomo. Los análisis de sangre para detectar plomo se recomiendan generalmente para:

- Niños de 1 a 2 años de edad.
- Niños u otros miembros de la familia que hayan estado expuestos a niveles altos de plomo.
- Niños que deben examinarse en virtud del plan local o estatal de exámenes médicos.

Su médico puede explicarle los resultados de las pruebas y decirle si es necesario realizar más análisis.

Otras fuentes de plomo

Plomo en el agua potable

Las fuentes más comunes de plomo en el agua potable son las tuberías, grifos y accesorios de plomo.

Las tuberías de plomo son más factibles de encontrar en las ciudades más antiguas y en las casas construidas antes de 1986.

El plomo en el agua potable no presenta ningún olor ni sabor.

Para saber con seguridad si tiene plomo en el agua potable, debe hacerla analizar.

Recuerde que las casas más viejas con un pozo privado también pueden tener materiales de plomería que contengan plomo.

Medidas que puede tomar para reducir el plomo en el agua potable

- Use solo agua fría para beber, cocinar y preparar la leche del bebé. Recuerde que hervir el agua no elimina el plomo de esta.
- Antes de beber el agua, deje corriendo el grifo para purgar las tuberías del hogar, tomando una ducha, lave la ropa sucia o lave los trastes.
- Limpie regularmente el filtro del grifo (también llamado aireador).
- Si usa un filtro certificado para eliminar el plomo, no olvide leer las instrucciones para aprender cuándo cambiar el cartucho. El uso de un filtro después de su vencimiento puede hacerlo menos eficaz en la eliminación del plomo.

Comuníquese con su empresa de suministro de agua para determinar si la tubería que conecta su casa a la cañería de agua principal (llamada línea de servicio) es de plomo. Su empresa de agua local también puede brindarle información sobre los niveles de plomo en el agua potable de su sistema.

Para obtener más información sobre el plomo en el agua potable, comuníquese con Línea directa de la EPA sobre el agua potable (en inglés) al **1-800-426-4791**. Si tiene otras preguntas sobre la prevención del envenenamiento por plomo, llame al **1-800 424-LEAD.***

Llame a su departamento de salud local o a su empresa de agua para averiguar cómo obtener un análisis del agua de su casa, o visite epa.gov/safewater para ver información de la EPA sobre el plomo en el agua potable. Algunos estados o empresas de servicios públicos ofrecen programas para pagar el análisis del agua de los residentes. Comuníquese con el servicio público de agua local o estatal para obtener más información.

* Las personas con dificultades del habla o la audición pueden acceder a este número a través de TTY llamando al Servicio Federal de Transmisión de Información al 1-800-877-8339.

13

95

Renovación, reparación o pintura

Si contrata a un contratista para que realice proyectos de renovación, reparación o pintura (RRP) en una casa o centro de cuidado infantil construidos antes de 1978 (como centros preescolares y jardines de infancia), el contratista debe:

- Ser una empresa certificada en prácticas seguras con el plomo, aprobada por la EPA o por un programa estatal autorizado por la EPA.

- Utilizar personas cualificadas y capacitadas (renovadores certificados en prácticas seguras con el plomo) que empleen prácticas de trabajo seguras con el plomo específicas, a fin de evitar la contaminación con plomo.

- Darle una copia del documento informativo de la EPA sobre peligros relacionados con el plomo que se titula *Guía de prácticas acreditas seguras para trabajar con el plomo para remodeler correctamente*.

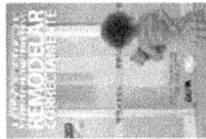

Los contratistas de RRP que trabajen en casas o centros de cuidado infantil construidos antes de 1978 deben seguir prácticas de trabajo seguras con el plomo que:

- **Contengan el área de trabajo.** Debe contenerse el área para que el polvo y los escombros no se escapen del área de trabajo. Deben colocarse letreros de advertencia, y debe usarse cinta y material plástico u otro tipo de material impermeable.

- **Eviten los métodos de renovación que generan grandes cantidades de polvo contaminado con plomo.** Algunos métodos producen tanto polvo contaminado con plomo que su uso está prohibido. Entre estos métodos se incluyen:

  - Quema o flameado a llama abierta.

  - Lijado, esmerilado, cepillado, uso de pistolas de aguja o limpieza a chorro con herramientas eléctricas y equipos sin cubierta y accesorio de aspiradora HEPA.

  - Pistola de aire caliente a temperaturas superiores a 1100 °F.

- **Limpien minuciosamente.** El área de trabajo debe limpiarse diariamente. Una vez terminado todo el trabajo, debe limpiarse el área con métodos de limpieza especiales.

- **Eliminen los desechos adecuadamente.** Recoja los residuos en una bolsa o lámina de alta resistencia y séllela. Cuando transporte los residuos, asegúrese de que la bolsa o lámina esté bien cerrada para que el polvo y los escombros no se escapen.

Para obtener más información sobre los requisitos de la EPA para los proyectos de RRP, visite epa.gov/getleadsafe o lea *Guía de prácticas acreditas seguras para trabajar con el plomo para remodeler correctamente*.

Dónde se encuentra la pintura con base de plomo

Generalmente, cuanto más vieja sea su casa o centro de cuidado infantil, mayor será la posibilidad de que tenga pintura con base de plomo.[1]

Muchas viviendas —incluidas las viviendas privadas, las de propiedad federal y las que reciben ayuda federal— y centros de cuidado infantil construidos antes de 1978 tienen pintura con base de plomo. En 1978, el gobierno federal prohibió el uso por parte del consumidor de pintura que contenga plomo.[2]

En la página 7, encontrará cómo establecer si la pintura tiene plomo.

El plomo puede encontrarse en:

- Casas y centros de cuidado infantil en la ciudad, el campo o los suburbios;

- Casas y apartamentos unifamiliares privados y públicos;

- Superficies dentro y fuera de la casa; y

- La tierra alrededor de la casa (la tierra puede acumular plomo de la pintura exterior u otras fuentes, tales como la gasolina con plomo que se usaba en el pasado en los automóviles).

Obtenga más información sobre dónde se encuentra plomo en epa.gov/lead.

---

[1] En la actualidad, el gobierno federal define la "pintura con base de plomo" como pintura con niveles de plomo superiores o iguales a 1.0 miligramo por centímetro cuadrado (mg/cm) o con más de 0.5 % por peso.

[2] En la actualidad, el gobierno federal define la "pintura que contiene plomo" como plomo en pintura nueva seca que supere las 90 partes por millón (ppm) por peso.

5

12

Reduciendo los peligros del plomo (continuación)

Si en su casa se realizó un trabajo para remover el plomo o si se trata de una vivienda que recibe ayuda federal, una vez que se termine el trabajo, deben realizarse las actividades de limpieza del polvo hasta que las pruebas de aprobación indiquen que los niveles de polvo de plomo están por debajo de los siguientes niveles:

- 40 microgramos por pie cuadrado ($\mu g/pie^2$) en pisos, incluidos pisos alfombrados.

- 250 $\mu g/pie^2$ en los antepechos de ventanas interiores.

- 400 $\mu g/pie^2$ en los canales de ventanas.

Para obtener ayuda para localizar en su área profesionales certificados que remuevan el plomo, llame a la agencia estatal o local (vea las páginas 14 y 15), visite epa.gov/lead o llame al **1-800-424-LEAD**.

Identificando la pintura con base de plomo y los peligros de la pintura con base de plomo

La pintura con base de plomo deteriorada (descascarada, picada, pulverizada, agrietada o dañada) es un peligro y requiere atención inmediata. La **pintura con base de plomo** también puede ser un peligro si se encuentra en superficies que los niños puedan morder o que se desgasten mucho, tales como:

- Ventanas y antepechos de ventanas.

- Puertas y marcos de puertas.

- Escaleras, pasamanos, barandas y porches.

La pintura con base de plomo generalmente no es peligrosa si está en buenas condiciones y no está en una superficie de impacto o de fricción, como en una ventana.

El polvo de plomo puede formarse al raspar, lijar o calentar la pintura con base de plomo. También se forma cuando las superficies pintadas que contienen polvo se golpean o frotan entre sí. Las partículas y el polvo de la pintura que contiene plomo pueden acumularse en superficies y objetos que las personas tocan. El polvo de plomo que se ha acumulado puede volver a mezclarse con el aire cuando se aspira o barre la casa, o cuando las personas caminan sobre el mismo. Actualmente, la EPA define como peligrosos los siguientes niveles de plomo en el polvo:

- 40 microgramos por pie cuadrado ($\mu g/pie^2$) o más en pisos, incluidos pisos alfombrados.

- 250 $\mu g/pie^2$ o más en los antepechos de ventanas interiores.

El plomo en la tierra puede ser peligroso cuando los niños juegan en tierra descubierta o cuando las personas meten tierra en la casa con los zapatos. Actualmente, la EPA define como peligrosos los siguientes niveles de plomo en la tierra:

- 400 partes por millón (ppm) o más en áreas de juego de tierra descubierta.

- 1,200 ppm (promedio) o más en la tierra descubierta del resto del jardín.

Recuerde que el plomo de las partículas de pintura —que puede ver— y el polvo de plomo —que tal vez no pueda ver— pueden ser peligrosos.

La única forma de saber si existe peligro debido a la presencia de plomo en pintura, polvo o tierra es realizando pruebas. En la página siguiente se describe cómo hacer esto.

6

Reduciendo los peligros del plomo

Alterar la pintura con base de plomo o remover incorrectamente el plomo puede aumentar el peligro para su familia, ya que esparce aún más el polvo de plomo en la casa.

- Además de la limpieza diaria y la buena nutrición, usted puede reducir **temporariamente** los riesgos relacionados con la pintura con base de plomo tomando medidas, como la reparación de las superficies pintadas que estén dañadas y plantar césped para cubrir la tierra contaminada con plomo. Estas medidas no son soluciones permanentes y necesitarán atención continua.

- Para minimizar la exposición al plomo cuando renueve, repare o pinte su casa, contrate a un renovador certificado por el estado o la EPA que esté capacitado en el uso de prácticas de trabajo seguras con el plomo. Si es una persona que suele hacer los trabajos por su cuenta, aprenda a utilizar prácticas de trabajo seguras con el plomo en su casa.

- Para remover permanentemente los peligros relacionados con el plomo, debe contratar a un contratista certificado para que "remueva" el plomo. Los métodos para remover (o eliminar permanentemente el peligro) incluyen la eliminación, el sellado o el revestimiento de la pintura con base de plomo con materiales especiales. Simplemente pintar sobre la pintura que presenta riesgos con una pintura común no es un control permanente.

Siempre recurra a un contratista certificado que esté capacitado para corregir los peligros relacionados con el plomo de manera segura.

- Contrate a una empresa certificada en prácticas seguras con el plomo (vea la página 12) para realizar proyectos de renovación, reparación o pintura (RRP) a fin de no alterar las superficies pintadas.

- Para corregir permanentemente los peligros relacionados con el plomo, contrate a un profesional certificado para que "remueva" el plomo. Esto asegurará que el contratista sepa cómo trabajar en forma segura y tenga el equipo apropiado para limpiar minuciosamente.

Los contratistas certificados contratarán a trabajadores cualificados y seguirán reglas estrictas de seguridad según lo dicta el estado o el gobierno federal.

10

Verificando si su casa tiene plomo

Puede evaluar su casa de diferentes maneras para determinar si tiene plomo:

- Una **inspección** de la pintura con base de plomo le dirá si su casa tiene pintura con base de plomo y dónde se localiza. Sin embargo, esta inspección no le dirá si en su casa existen actualmente peligros relacionados con el plomo. Un profesional experto en pruebas capacitado y certificado, que se llama inspector de pintura con base de plomo, realizará la inspección de la pintura utilizando métodos como:

  - Máquina portátil de fluorescencia por rayos X (XRF, por sus siglas en inglés).

  - Pruebas de laboratorio de muestras de pintura.

- Una **evaluación de riesgo** le dirá si en su casa existe actualmente algún peligro relacionado con el plomo debido a la presencia de plomo en la pintura, el polvo o la tierra. También le dirá qué acciones debe llevar a cabo para eliminar estos peligros. Un profesional experto en pruebas capacitado y certificado, que se llama asesor de riesgo, hará lo siguiente:

  - Tomará muestras de la pintura deteriorada de puertas, ventanas, pisos, escaleras y paredes.

  - Tomará muestras del polvo cerca de las superficies pintadas y muestras de tierra descubierta del patio.

  - Hará pruebas de laboratorio con las muestras de pintura, polvo y tierra.

- Una combinación de evaluación de riesgo e inspección le dirá si en su casa hay pintura con base de plomo, si existe algún peligro relacionado con el plomo y dónde se localizan ambos.

Asegúrese de leer el informe que le entreguen una vez finalizada la inspección o la evaluación de riesgo, y pregunte todo lo que no entienda.

7

98

Verificando si su casa tiene plomo (continuación)

Al preparar un trabajo de renovación, reparación o pintura en una casa construida antes de 1978, los renovadores certificados para prácticas seguras con el plomo (vea la página 12) pueden:

- Tomar muestras de partículas de pintura para determinar si hay pintura con base de plomo en el área que se prevé renovar y enviarlas para analizar a un laboratorio especializado en plomo reconocido por la EPA. En viviendas que reciben ayuda federal, la persona que recolecte estas muestras debe ser un evaluador de riesgo o inspector certificado de pintura con base de plomo.

- Utilizar juegos de pruebas reconocidos por la EPA para determinar si no hay pintura con base de plomo (no se deben usar en viviendas que reciban ayuda federal).

- Suponer que hay pintura con base de plomo y utilizar prácticas de trabajo seguras con el plomo.

Existen programas estatales y federales para garantizar que las pruebas se realicen de modo seguro, confiable y con eficacia. Comuníquese con la agencia estatal o local para obtener más información, visite epa.gov/lead o llame al **1-800-424-LEAD (5323)** para obtener una lista de contactos en su área.[3]

---

[3] Las personas con impedimentos auditivos o del habla pueden acceder a este número a través del sistema TTY llamando al Federal Relay Service (Servicio Federal de Retransmisión) al 1-800-877-8399.

Lo que usted puede hacer en estos momentos para proteger a su familia

Si sospecha que su casa tiene algún peligro relacionado con pintura con base de plomo, puede tomar algunas medidas inmediatas para reducir el riesgo de su familia:

- Si alquila, infórmele al propietario si hay pintura descascarándose o picándose.

- Mantenga las superficies pintadas limpias y sin polvo. Limpie semanalmente los pisos, los marcos y antepechos de las ventanas y las demás superficies. Use un trapeador o una esponja con agua tibia y un limpiador para usos múltiples. (Recuerde: nunca mezcle productos de amoníaco con blanqueadores, ya que pueden formar gases peligrosos.)

- Limpie inmediatamente y con cuidado las partículas de pintura sin generar polvo.

- Enjuague bien y con frecuencia las esponjas y las cabezas de los trapeadores mientras limpia las áreas sucias o con polvo, y vuelva a hacerlo cuando termine de limpiar.

- Lávese con frecuencia las manos y también las de sus hijos, especialmente antes de comer, antes de la siesta y antes de irse a dormir.

- Mantenga limpias las áreas de juego. Lave con regularidad los biberones, los chupones, los juguetes y los animales de peluche.

- No permita que los niños muerdan los antepechos de las ventanas ni las demás superficies pintadas, ni tampoco que coman tierra.

- Al realizar renovaciones, reparaciones o pintura, contrate a empresas de renovación certificadas en prácticas seguras con el plomo aprobadas por el estado o la EPA (vea la página 12).

- Límpiese o quítese los zapatos antes de entrar a la casa para evitar meter el plomo de la tierra.

- Asegúrese de que los niños coman alimentos nutritivos, bajos en grasa y altos en hierro y calcio, tales como las espinacas y los productos lácteos. Los niños con una dieta adecuada absorben menos plomo.

Mold Prevention and Control Addendum to Lease Agreement

This Addendum is entered into by and between _____,

"Owner/Agent" and _____, "Resident."

Resident is renting from Owner the "Premises" located at: _____

_____

This Addendum is incorporated into the Lease Agreement between Lessor and Lessee, and this Addendum controls in the event of conflict with the Lease Agreement. The term of this Addendum will begin on the commencement date set forth in this Addendum and end on the expiration date set forth in the Lease Agreement unless otherwise provided in this Addendum or subsequent writing(s). If the Lease Agreement ends, this Addendum will end at the same time. This Addendum supersedes any oral or prior written agreement regarding mold. The Parties acknowledge that no representation, inducements, promises, or agreements have been made by or on behalf of any party, except those covenants and agreements in this written agreement. Where context requires, the singular will include the plural, the plural the singular, and genders will include all genders. All Federal, State, and local laws apply where omitted.

MOLD. Mold consists of naturally occurring microscopic organisms which reproduce by spores. Mold breaks down and feeds on organic matter in the environment. The mold spores spread through the air and the combination of excessive moisture and organic matter allows for mold growth. Not all, but certain types and amounts of mold can lead to adverse health effects and/or allergic reactions. Not all mold is readily visible, but when it is, can often be seen in the form of discoloration, ranging from white to orange and from green to brown and black, and often there is a musty odor present. Reducing moisture and proper housekeeping significantly reduces the chance of mold and mold growth.

In consideration of the mutual promises, Owner and Resident agree as follows:

1. **CLIMATE CONTROL.** Resident agree to use air-conditioning and heating, if provided, in a reasonable manner to keep the Premises properly ventilated by periodically opening windows to allow for circulation of fresh air during dry weather.

2. **MOISTURE ACCUMULATION.** Resident will remove visible moisture accumulation in or on the Premises, including windows, walls, ceilings, floors, and all other surfaces as soon as reasonably possible after occurrence. Resident agrees to use exhaust fans (where applicable) when cooking and in the bathroom (if available) before, during, and after showers. Resident agrees to keep climate and moisture in the Premises at reasonable levels.

3. **PREMISES CLEANLINESS.** Resident agrees to keep the Premises clean, particularly in the kitchen, bathrooms, carpets, and floors, including vacuuming regularly, mopping floors, and using household cleaner on hard surfaces. It is important to remove dirt and debris that can harbor mold.

4. **NOTIFY OWNER.** In order to remedy or repair the situation as necessary, promptly notify the Owner in writing if any of the following occur:

   a. A water leak, excessive moisture or standing water on the Premises.

   b. A water leak, excessive moisture of standing water in a common area, including the Resident's self-storage area (if any).

c. Mold growth in or on the Premises that persists after Resident has attempted several times to remove with household cleaners (e.g., Lysol, Pine-Sol, Tilex Mildew Remover, Clorox Cleanup, bleach-water combination).

d. Any air conditioning, heating, or ventilation system problems that are discovered or readily discoverable.

e. AVOIDING MOLD GROWTH: In order to avoid mold growth, it is important to avoid excessive moisture build-up in the Premises. Prolonged moisture can result from various sources, such as leaking windows and doors, bathroom, washer/dryer, dehumidifier, refrigerator overflow, plumbing leaks, washer/dryer leaks, spills, shower stalls, and bath floors.

5. **TREATING MOLDS ON NON-POROUS SURFACES.** It is recommended that Resident first clean the area with soap and water (always apply cleaner in an area five or six times larger than the visible mold area). Allow it to dry thoroughly. Within twenty-four (24) hours, apply a pre-mixed household biocide (e.g., Lysol, Pine-Sol, Tilex Mildew Remover, Clorox Cleanup). Be sure to follow directions on packaging and wear appropriate safety equipment to protect skins, eyes, and clothing. Not all cleaners kill mold. Tilex or Clorox contain bleach, which can discolor and stain. Do **NOT** apply biocides to porous areas.

6. **INSPECTIONS.** Resident agrees that Owner may conduct inspections of the Premises at any time with reasonable notice.

7. **TERMINATION OF TENANCY.** Owner reserves the right to terminate the Lease Agreement and Resident agrees to vacate the Premises in the event Owner in its sole judgment feels that either there is mold or mildew present in the Premises which may pose a safety or health hazard to persons.

8. **VIOLATION OF LEASE AGREEMENT.** Non-compliance of this Addendum will be deemed a violation under terms of the Lease Agreement.

9. **REMEDY FOR VIOLATION.** Any violation of this Addendum constitutes a material breach of the Lease Agreement and allows the Owner to exercise any default remedies permitted in the Lease Agreement, including termination of the Lease Agreement, in accordance with local and State laws. Failure to cure a material breach of the Lease Agreement may result in the filing of an Unlawful Detainer (Eviction) action against the Resident. If an Unlawful Detainer action is filed against the Resident, it could result in a judgment against the Resident which may include monetary amounts, attorneys' fees, and other court costs. Once a lawsuit is filed with the Court, it may become a public record and may later appear on the Resident's Credit Report and may have an adverse impact on the Resident's Credit Rating. This could seriously affect the Resident's ability to obtain future credit, including future rentals. This clause is not be interpreted to restrict the Owner's rights to terminate the Lease Agreement for any lawful reason.

10. **RESIDENT LIABILITY.** The Resident is responsible and liable for any and all losses, damages, and fines that the Owner incurs as a result of the Resident's violations of the terms of this Addendum. Further, the Resident agrees that the Resident is responsible for and will be held liable for any and all actions of any persons who occupy the Premises in violation of the terms of this Addendum, e.g., property damage, disturbance of other residents, violence, and attempted violence on another person. In accordance with applicable laws, without limiting the Resident's liability, the Resident agrees the Owner will have the right to collect against any renter's or liability insurance policy maintained by the Renter for any losses or damages that the Owner incurs as the result of any violations of this Addendum.

11. **INDEMNIFICATION.** Resident agree to defend, indemnify, and hold harmless Owner from future actions, claims, damages, loss, injuries, attorneys' fees, and costs resulting from the action or inaction of the Resident, other occupants, and Resident's guests, agents, and invitees in cleaning and maintaining or failure or Resident to timely report conditions to the Owner.

12. **SEVERABILITY.** If any provision of this Addendum is invalid or unenforceable under applicable law, such provision will be ineffective to the extent of such invalidity or unenforceability only without invalidating or otherwise affecting the remainder of this Addendum. The court will interpret this Addendum and provisions in a manner as to uphold the valid portions of this Addendum while preserving the intent of the Parties.

Comments: _____

_____

_____

_____

_____

_____

_____

_____

_____

_____

_____

_____

_____

_____

_____

_____

_____

By signing below, Resident confirms that he/she has received, reviewed, and understands this Addendum.

_____	_____	_____	_____
Resident/Lessee	Date	Resident/Lessee	Date
_____	_____	_____	_____
Resident/Lessee	Date	Resident/Lessee	Date
_____	_____	_____	_____
Owner/Lessor or Owner Agent/ Lessor Agent	Date	Owner/Lessor or Owner Agent/ Lessor Agent	Date

Pest Control Disclosure Notice Addendum to Lease Agreement

CAUTION – PESTICIDES ARE TOXIC CHEMICALS

This Addendum is entered into by and between _____,

"Owner/Agent" and _____, "Resident."

Resident is renting from Owner the "Premises" located at: _____

_____

This Addendum is incorporated into the Lease Agreement between Lessor and Lessee, and this Addendum controls in the event of conflict with the Lease Agreement. The term of this Addendum will begin on the commencement date set forth in this Addendum and end on the expiration date set forth in the Lease Agreement unless otherwise provided in this Addendum or subsequent writing(s). This Addendum supersedes all oral and prior written agreements regarding pest control. The Parties acknowledge that no representation, inducements, promises, or agreements have been made by or on behalf of any party, except those covenants and agreements in this written agreement. Where context requires, the singular will include the plural, the plural the singular, and genders will include all genders. All Federal, State, and local laws apply where omitted.

STRUCTURAL PEST CONTROL COMPANIES. Structural Pest Control Companies are registered by the Structural Pest Control Board and apply pesticides which are registered and approved for use by State health departments of pesticide regulation and the U.S. Environmental Protection Agency (EPA). Registration is granted when the State finds that based on existing scientific evidence there are no appreciable risks if proper use conditions were followed or that the risks are outweighed by the benefits. The degree of risk depends on the degree of exposure, so exposure should be minimized however possible.

If, within 24 hours after move-in, anyone in the Premises experiences symptoms similar to common seasonal illness comparable to the flu, contact a physician, poison control center, and the pest control company, immediately. Contact the Owner only after these immediate actions have been taken.

For further information on the dangers of pesticides, contact: _____

_____

In consideration of the mutual promises, Owner and Resident agree as follows:

1. **PRIOR INSPECTION OF PREMISES.** Resident has inspected the Premises and reported any pest infestation at move-in. Resident confirms that there are no pests in the Premises on move-in.

2. **PRIOR INSPECTION OF PERSONAL PROPERTY BROUGHT ONTO THE PREMISES.** Resident promises all personal property (e.g., furniture, clothing, mattress, bedding, rugs) that Resident brings onto the Premises have been inspected and do not contain pests. Resident agrees to carefully inspect all personal property brought onto the Premises prior to entering the Premises to ensure that the property is pest free. If the Resident detects that any personal property of the Resident may have pests, Resident promises not to bring that property onto the Premises. Resident agrees to do his/her part to ensure pests do not enter the Premises after he/she moves, including, but not limited to, continuing to check any personal property that is brought into the Premises for pests; checking all luggage, clothing, and other personal belongings for pests if Resident stays in a hotel or visits another

home; uses public transportation; or utilizes other public areas that may carry pests. In addition, Resident agrees to inspect furniture and personal belongings after guests visit or stay in the Premises to ensure no pests were brought onto the Premises by guest.

3. **COOPERATION.** To prevent and treat pest infestations, it is important for Owner and Resident to work together. Resident will cooperate with inspections to facilitate detection and treatment of pests, including providing requested information that is necessary to facilitate the detection and treatment of pests to the pest control operator.

4. **PREMISES CLEANLINESS.** Resident agrees to keep the Premises clean, particularly in the kitchen, bathrooms, carpets, and floors, including: vacuuming regularly, mopping floors, and using household cleaners on appropriate surfaces. It is important to remove food, dirt, and debris that can harbor pests. Resident will maintain a clean pest-free environment.

5. **NOTIFY OWNER.** Resident will notify the Owner immediately if there are any problems or signs of problems with pests.

6. **PEST CONTROL SERVICES.** Owner will provide pest control services, either directly or through a contractor. Resident agrees to allow Owner, without interference, to engage in chemical and mechanical pest control measures within the Premises and grounds of the Premises.

7. **NO GUARANTEES.** Owner makes no guarantee to provide Resident with alternative housing due to pest control issues as long as the issue is resolved within a reasonable time frame as determined solely be the Owner. Owner makes no guarantee to provide a pest-free environment, but will take reasonable steps toward this goal.

8. **NOTICE TO TREAT PREMISES.** Resident will receive at least 24 hours prior written notice with instructions for preparing the Premises for treatment as necessary.

9. **COOPERATION.** Resident agrees to fully cooperate with Owner Landlord, pest control service, and properly prepare the Premises as necessary.

10. **REMEDIES FOR NOT PREPARING PREMISES.** If the Premises are not ready and treatment is necessary, or Owner or pest control personnel must prepare the Premises for treatment, a minimum rate of $ _____/hour preparation fee will be assessed to Resident for failure to properly prepare the Premises.

11. **INSPECTIONS.** Resident agree that Owner may conduct inspections of the Premises at any time with reasonable notice.

12. **TERMINATION OF TENANCY.** Owner reserves the right to terminate the Lease Agreement and Resident agrees to vacate the Premises in the event Owner in its sole judgment feels the Premises may pose a safety or health hazard.

13. **VIOLATION OF LEASE AGREEMENT.** Non-compliance of this Addendum will be deemed a violation under terms of the Lease Agreement.

14. **REMEDY FOR VIOLATION.** Any violation of this Addendum constitutes a material breach of the Lease Agreement and allows the Owner to exercise any default remedies permitted in the Lease Agreement, including termination of the Lease Agreement, in accordance with local and State laws. Failure to cure a material breach of the Lease Agreement may result in the filing of an Unlawful Detainer (Eviction) action against the Resident. If an Unlawful Detainer action is filed

against the Resident, it could result in a judgment against the Resident which may include monetary amounts, attorneys' fees, and other court costs. Once a lawsuit is filed with the Court, it may become a public record and may later appear on the Resident's Credit Report and may have an adverse impact on the Resident's Credit Rating. This could seriously affect the Resident's ability to obtain future credit, including future rentals. This clause is not be interpreted to restrict the Owner's rights to terminate the Lease Agreement for any lawful reason.

15. **RESIDENT LIABILITY.** The Resident is responsible and liable for any and all losses, damages, and fines that the Owner incurs as a result of the Resident's violations of the terms of this Addendum. Further, the Resident agrees that the Resident is responsible for and will be held liable for any and all actions of any persons who occupy the Premises in violation of the terms of this Addendum, e.g., property damage, disturbance of other residents, violence, and attempted violence on another person. In accordance with applicable laws, without limiting the Resident's liability, the Resident agrees the Owner will have the right to collect against any renter's or liability insurance policy maintained by the Renter for any losses or damages that the Owner incurs as the result of any violations of this Addendum.

16. **INDEMNIFICATION.** Resident agree to defend, indemnify, and hold harmless Owner from future actions, claims, damages, loss, injuries, attorneys' fees, and costs resulting from the action or inaction of the Resident, other occupants, and Resident's guests, agents, and invitees in cleaning and maintaining or failure or Resident to timely report conditions to the Owner.

17. **SEVERABILITY.** If any provision of this Addendum is invalid or unenforceable under applicable law, such provision will be ineffective to the extent of such invalidity or unenforceability only without invalidating or otherwise affecting the remainder of this Addendum. The court will interpret this Addendum and provisions in a manner as to uphold the valid portions of this Addendum while preserving the intent of the Parties.

Comments: _____

_____

_____

_____

_____

_____

By signing below, Resident confirms that he/she has received, reviewed, and understands this Addendum.

_____	_____	_____	_____
Resident/Lessee	Date	Resident/Lessee	Date
_____	_____	_____	_____
Resident/Lessee	Date	Resident/Lessee	Date
_____	_____	_____	_____
Owner/Lessor or Owner Agent/ Lessor Agent	Date	Owner/Lessor or Owner Agent/ Lessor Agent	Date

Bed Bug Addendum to Lease Agreement

This Addendum is entered into by and between _____,

"Owner/Agent" and _____, "Resident."

Resident is renting from Owner the "Premises" located at: _____

_____

This Addendum is incorporated into the Lease Agreement between Lessor and Lessee, and this Addendum controls in the event of conflict with the Lease Agreement. The term of this Addendum will begin on the commencement date set forth in this Addendum and end on the expiration date set forth in the Lease Agreement unless otherwise provided in this Addendum or subsequent writing(s). This Addendum supersedes all oral and prior written agreements regarding bed bugs. The Parties acknowledge that no representation, inducements, promises, or agreements have been made by or on behalf of any party, except those covenants and agreements in this written agreement. Where context requires, the singular will include the plural, the plural the singular, and genders will include all genders. All Federal, State, and local laws apply where omitted.

BED BUG APPEARANCE. Bed bugs have six legs. Adult bed bugs have flat bodies about 1/4 of an inch in length. Their color can vary from red and brown to copper colored. Young bed bugs are very small. Their bodies are about 1/16 of an inch in length. They have almost no color. When a bed bug feeds, its body swells, may lengthen, and becomes bright red, sometimes making it appear to be a different insect. Bed bugs do not fly. They can either crawl or be carried from place to place on objects, people, or animals. Bed bugs can be hard to find and identify because they are tiny and try to stay hidden.

LIFE CYCLE AND REPRODUCTION. An average bed bug lives for about 10 months. Female bed bugs lay one to five eggs per day. Bed bugs grow to full adulthood in about 21 days. Bed bugs can survive for months without feeding. **Bed Bug Bites:** Because bed bugs usually feed at night, most people are bitten in their sleep and do not realize they were bitten. A person's reaction to insect bites is an immune response and so varies from person to person. Sometimes the red welts caused by the bites will not be noticed until many days after a person was bitten, if at all.

Common signs and symptoms of a possible bed bug infestation:

- Small red to reddish brown fecal spots on mattresses, box springs, bed frames, mattresses, linens, upholstery, or walls.

- Molted bed bug skin, white-sticky eggs, or empty eggshells.

- Very heavily infested areas may have a characteristically sweet odor.

- Red, itchy bite marks, especially on the legs, arms, and other body parts exposed while sleeping. However, some people do not show bed bug lesions on their bodies even though bed bugs may have fed on them.

For more information about bed bugs, see the Internet websites of the U.S. Environmental Protection Agency (www.epa.gov/bedbugs/) and the National Pest Management Association (www.npmapestworld.org/).

In consideration of the mutual promises, Owner and Resident agree as follows:

1. **PRIOR INSPECTION OF PREMISES.** Resident has inspected the Premises and reported any bed bug infestation at move-in. Resident confirms that there are no bed bugs at move-in.

2. **PRIOR INSPECTION OF PERSONAL PROPERTY BROUGHT ONTO THE PREMISES.** Resident promises all personal property (e.g., furniture, clothing, mattress, bedding, rugs) that Resident brings onto the Premises have been inspected and do not contain bed bugs. Resident agrees to carefully inspect all personal property brought onto the Premises prior to entering the Premises to ensure that the property is bed-bugs-free. If the Resident detects that any personal property of the Resident may have bed bugs, Resident promises not to bring that property onto the Premises. Resident agrees to do his/her part to ensure bed bugs do not enter the Premises after he/she moves, including, but not limited to, continuing to check any personal property that is brought into the Premises for bed bugs; checking all luggage, clothing, and other personal belongings for bed bugs if Resident stays in a hotel or visits another home; uses public transportation; or utilizes other public areas that may carry bed bugs. In addition, Resident agrees to inspect furniture and personal belongings after guests visit or stay in the Premises to ensure no bed bugs were brought onto the Premises by guest.

3. **COOPERATION.** To prevent and treat bed bug infestations, it is important for Owner and Resident to work together. Resident will cooperate with inspections to facilitate detection and treatment of bed bugs, including providing requested information that is necessary to facilitate the detection and treatment of bed bugs to the pest control operator.

4. **NOTIFICATION REQUIREMENT.** Early detection and reporting of bed bugs are important components required for preventing bed bug infestations. Resident will notify the Owner immediately if there are any problems or signs of problems with bed bugs. Resident are to provide: 1) description of what was discovered; 2) date/time infestation was discovered; 3) location of infestation; 4) name, address, and contact; and 5) possible infestation source.

5. **NO GUARANTEES.** Owner makes no guarantee to provide Resident with alternative housing due to bed bug issues as long as the issue is resolved within a reasonable time frame as determined solely be the Owner. Owner makes no guarantee to provide a bed bug -free environment, but will take reasonable steps toward this goal.

6. **NOTICE TO TREAT PREMISES.** Resident will receive at least 24 hours prior written notice with instructions for preparing the Premises for treatment as necessary.

7. **COOPERATION.** Resident agrees to fully cooperate with Owner Landlord, pest control service, and properly prepare the Premises as necessary.

8. **REMEDIES FOR NOT PREPARING PREMISES.** If the Premises are not ready and treatment is necessary, or Owner or pest control personnel must prepare the Premises for treatment, a minimum rate of $_____ /hour preparation fee will be assessed to Resident for failure to properly prepare the Premises.

9. **INSPECTIONS.** Resident agree that Owner may conduct inspections of the Premises at any time with reasonable notice.

10. **TERMINATION OF TENANCY.** Owner reserves the right to terminate the Lease Agreement and Resident agrees to vacate the Premises in the event Owner in its sole judgment feels the Premises may pose a safety or health hazard.

11. **VIOLATION OF LEASE AGREEMENT.** Non-compliance of this Addendum will be deemed a violation under terms of the Lease Agreement.

12. **REMEDY FOR VIOLATION.** Any violation of this Addendum constitutes a material breach of the Lease Agreement and allows the Owner to exercise any default remedies permitted in the Lease Agreement, including termination of the Lease Agreement, in accordance with local and State laws. Failure to cure a material breach of the Lease Agreement may result in the filing of an Unlawful Detainer (Eviction) action against the Resident. If an Unlawful Detainer action is filed against the Resident, it could result in a judgment against the Resident which may include monetary amounts, attorneys' fees, and other court costs. Once a lawsuit is filed with the Court, it may become a public record and may later appear on the Resident's Credit Report and may have an adverse impact on the Resident's Credit Rating. This could seriously affect the Resident's ability to obtain future credit, including future rentals. This clause is not be interpreted to restrict the Owner's rights to terminate the Lease Agreement for any lawful reason.

13. **RESIDENT LIABILITY.** The Resident is responsible and liable for any and all losses, damages, and fines that the Owner incurs as a result of the Resident's violations of the terms of this Addendum. Further, the Resident agrees that the Resident is responsible for and will be held liable for any and all actions of any persons who occupy the Premises in violation of the terms of this Addendum, e.g., property damage, disturbance of other residents, violence, and attempted violence on another person. In accordance with applicable laws, without limiting the Resident's liability, the Resident agrees the Owner will have the right to collect against any renter's or liability insurance policy maintained by the Renter for any losses or damages that the Owner incurs as the result of any violations of this Addendum.

14. **INDEMNIFICATION.** Resident agree to defend, indemnify, and hold harmless Owner from future actions, claims, damages, loss, injuries, attorneys' fees, and costs resulting from the action or inaction of the Resident, other occupants, and Resident's guests, agents, and invitees in cleaning and maintaining or failure or Resident to timely report conditions to the Owner.

15. **SEVERABILITY.** If any provision of this Addendum is invalid or unenforceable under applicable law, such provision will be ineffective to the extent of such invalidity or unenforceability only without invalidating or otherwise affecting the remainder of this Addendum. The court will interpret this Addendum and provisions in a manner as to uphold the valid portions of this Addendum while preserving the intent of the Parties.

Comments: _____

_____

_____

_____

_____

_____

_____

_____

_____

By signing below, Resident confirms that he/she has received, reviewed, and understands this Addendum.

_____	_____	_____	_____
Resident/Lessee	Date	Resident/Lessee	Date
_____	_____	_____	_____
Resident/Lessee	Date	Resident/Lessee	Date
_____	_____	_____	_____
Owner/Lessor or Owner Agent/ Lessor Agent	Date	Owner/Lessor or Owner Agent/ Lessor Agent	Date

Satellite, Television, and Internet Dish/Antenna Installation Policy and Rules Addendum to Lease Agreement

This Addendum is entered into by and between _____,

"Owner/Agent" and _____, "Resident."

Resident is renting from Owner the "Premises" located at: _____

_____

This Addendum is incorporated into the Lease Agreement between Lessor and Lessee, and this Addendum controls in the event of conflict with the Lease Agreement. The term of this Addendum will begin on the commencement date set forth in this Addendum and end on the expiration date set forth in the Lease Agreement unless otherwise provided in this Addendum or subsequent writing(s). This Addendum supersedes all oral and prior written agreements regarding satellite, television, and Internet dish/antenna installation policy and rules. The Parties acknowledge that no representation, inducements, promises, or agreements have been made by or on behalf of any party, except those covenants and agreements in this written agreement. Where context requires, the singular will include the plural, the plural the singular, and genders will include all genders. All Federal, State, and local laws apply where omitted.

Residents have a limited right to install a transmitting or receiving satellite, tv, or Internet dish or receiving antenna, subject to FCC limitations. The Owner may impose reasonable restrictions as a condition of installing and using such equipment, and this Addendum contains the restrictions that the Owner and Resident agree to follow. Resident understands and agrees that not all residents will be able to receive satellite signals depending on the orientation of buildings and obstructions, and the Resident's failure to receive such signals will **NOT** be the basis for any reduction in rent or the basis for any early termination of the Lease Agreement. When the Resident considers satellite, TV, or Internet dish/antenna service(s), the Owner encourages the Resident to keep in mid the legal covenants in this Addendum as well as to the aesthetics of the Premises. *Resident will be liable for safety of other persons and property regarding any and all damages and/or injuries caused by the installation or use of the device(s) and/or equipment(s).* For these reasons, Owner highly recommends that before Resident commits to a contract, Resident confirms through the retailer or installer exactly how and where the device or equipment will need to be placed in order to receive high quality, interference-free reception that will be safe and avoid damage.

The following polices and rules are adopted by the parties and enforced to ensure Resident compliance with Federal, state, and local safety codes, rules, and regulations adopted to protect the safety of other residents or invitees, and to prevent damage to the property.

In consideration of the mutual promises, Owner and Resident agree as follows:

1. **INSTALLATION PLAN.** Although an installation plan is not required by the FCC rules for Over-the-Air-Reception-Devices (OTARD), the Owner highly recommends that the Resident submit a written plan for the location and installation of the device to the Owner prior to installation, in an effort to minimize forced removal of the device for improper installation. The plan will specify:

    a. A proposed location of the device, method and manner of installation, and the name, address, and telephone number of the Installer. Devices that both receive and transmit RF signals must be labeled with required hazard warnings and must comply with FCC and all Federal health and safety agency RF exposure limits and will only be installed by a professional installers to minimize the possibility that the device will be placed in a location that is likely to expose persons to the transmit signal at close proximity and for an extended period of time.

b. The nature, source, and manner of all electrical power to be connected to the device and the method of transmission of signal into the Premises or to the receiving appliance.

c. The type, size, and nature of all fastening devices to be used to secure the device to prevent it from falling, tipping, or injuring persons or property.

d. What measures will be taken during installation and regular use of the device to prevent structural damage to the building or property.

Following the submission of the installation plan, the Owner or its agents will set-up a meeting with the Resident, if necessary, to review the installation plan and method of installation.

2. **NOTIFICATION REQUIREMENT.** Resident is required to notify the Owner in writing prior to any installation. The notice must include a description of the location and method for the installation devise or equipment. As noted below, **NO holes may be made through any part of the property.**

3. **NUMBER AND SIZE.** Resident may install only <u>one</u> satellite dish or antenna within the Premises that Resident has exclusive use. A satellite dish may not exceed one meter (3.3 feet) in diameter, measured diagonally. An antenna or dish may receive, but not transmit signals.

4. **LOCATION AND INSTALLATION.** Resident is permitted to install individual satellite dishes or antennas to the extent and in locations allowed by local, State, and Federal laws. The installation, repair, and maintenance of the device must be done in a competent, workmanlike, and safe manner. Electrical wiring may only be done with prior written consent of the Owner and must be performed by a licensed electrician.

OWNER MUST BE PRESENT AT ALL INSTALLATIONS AND HAS THE FINAL SAY ON WHETHER AN INSTALLER DRILLS HOLES OF ANY SIZE OR SIMPLY PASSES CABLES UNDER WINDOWS OR DOORS.

The device, and any wiring, **may only be located within the boundaries of an area where the Resident is given "exclusive use and possession"** under the terms of the Lease Agreement. This means the device must be placed entirely within the Premises unless the Resident has the exclusive use of an enclosed patio or balcony, where such device may also be located within the boundaries of the patio or balcony. **The patio and balcony boundary of Resident's "exclusive use and possession" ends at the termination of the slab or deck area and the height of the top of the door or sliding door. The device and its wiring may not extend beyond these boundaries, nor protrude out of any window or over any fence or balcony railing.**

The device and its wiring will not be attached or located in any common areas, walkways, or any restricted or prohibited use or access areas of the Premises, e.g., roof, exterior walls. Installation of the device can only be done by the use of approved clamps or clamping devices, and weighted support stands. **No holes may be made through any wall, door, celling, floor,**

molding, casement, flashing, railing, window, or any other structure of the Premises or any other part. No damage to the Premises, building, or property is permitted, and if such damage occurs, the Resident is liable for the costs of all damages, repairs, and replacements. Failure of the Resident to pay for damages, repairs, and replacements may be the basis for the Owner's termination of the Lease Agreement as provided by law. No device may be located within 10 feet of a power line. Changes to the existing device already installed require a new installation plan.

5. **RECEPTION.** Signal transmission between the device and its appliances can be accomplished through one of the following two methods:

    a. Hardwire from the dish/antenna to the appliance using a "quick disconnect" connector. The coaxial cable or transmission line can then enter the Premises through a partially opened door or slider door during use and easily disconnected when not in use.

    b. Remove wireless transmitter that sends the signal from the dish/antenna to a receiver located next to the receiving appliance(s).

6. **MAINTENANCE.** The Resident will have the sole responsibility for maintaining the satellite dish or antenna and all related equipment.

7. **APPROVAL REVOCATION.** The Owner's allowance or approval to install a satellite, TV, or Internet dish/antenna on or around the Premises is subject to reversal or revocation upon 30 days' notice to Resident to remove the device or equipment, pursuant to local laws, if the governmental rules or regulations mandating allowance of the devices in residential rental properties is revised, revoked, overruled, withdrawn, or held unconstitutional.

8. **FINANCIAL PENALTY. In the event the Resident installs a satellite, TV, or Internet dish/antenna illegally, Owner has the option to enforce a $1,000.00 fine on the Resident.**

9. **LIABILITY INSURANCE AND INDEMNITY.** The Resident is responsible for any injury or damage to persons and property caused by either their satellite dish or its installation. Residents are required to purchase and maintain liability for the use of a satellite dish, which must name the Owner as an additional insured as well as an "interested party." The Resident will provide the Owner with proof of liability insurance prior to installation. The insurance coverage must be no less than $_____ and **MUST** remain in force while the satellite dish or antenna remains installed. The Resident agrees to defend, indemnify and hold Owner harmless of all claims by others not a party to this Addendum or Lease Agreement.

10. **APPLICABLE LAWS.** These rules are meant to comply with 47 C.F.R. § 1.4000 "Restrictions impairing reception of television broadcast signals, direct broadcast satellite services or multichannel multipoint distribution services," as they may be amended. All requirements of the Section are incorporated in this Addendum. The Resident will not have more rights to install or maintain satellite dishes under this Installation Policy than are allowed under 47 C.F.R. § 1.4000. In the event any portion of this Addendum is held to conflict with applicable law, those portions of the Lease Agreement will be deemed stricken and all other portions of this Addendum will remain in effect. No portion of this Addendum may be waived by the Owner or changed verbally. Any such waiver or change will be effective only when in writing and signed by the Owner.

11. **VACATING.** When vacating the Premises, Resident must make all repairs at Resident's expense and restore the Premises to its original condition, e.g. removal of the device, wiring, fixtures. An additional deposit may be required to ensure repairs are completed.

Comments: _____

_____

_____

_____

_____

_____

_____

_____

_____

_____

By signing below, Resident confirms that he/she has received, reviewed, and understands this Addendum.

_____	_____	_____	_____
Resident/Lessee	Date	Resident/Lessee	Date
_____	_____	_____	_____
Resident/Lessee	Date	Resident/Lessee	Date
_____	_____	_____	_____
Owner/Lessor or Owner Agent/ Lessor Agent	Date	Owner/Lessor or Owner Agent/ Lessor Agent	Date

Construction Addendum to Lease Agreement

This Addendum is entered into by and between _____,

"Owner/Agent" and _____, "Resident."

Resident is renting from Owner the "Premises" located at: _____

_____

This Addendum is incorporated into the Lease Agreement between Lessor and Lessee, and this Addendum controls in the event of conflict with the Lease Agreement. The term of this Addendum will begin on the commencement date set forth in this Addendum and end on the expiration date set forth in the Lease Agreement unless otherwise provided in this Addendum or subsequent writing(s). This Addendum supersedes all oral and prior written agreements regarding construction. The Parties acknowledge that no representation, inducements, promises, or agreements have been made by or on behalf of any party, except those covenants and agreements in this written agreement. All state, and local laws apply if omitted. In consideration of the mutual promises, Owner and Resident agree as follows:

Resident understands and agrees that the Premises may occasionally be under construction and agrees to hold Owner harmless and to indemnify Owner against any and all liability arising from construction traffic, dust, construction equipment, temporary utility outages, etc.

All parties understand that the Resident will not be compensated for any unforeseen delays. If Resident chooses to cancel for any reason, other than for construction delays, all termination charges will apply according the Lease Agreement.

Comments: _____

_____

_____

_____

_____

_____

_____

_____

By signing below, Resident confirms that he/she has received, reviewed, and understands this Addendum.

_____	_____	_____	_____
Resident/Lessee	Date	Resident/Lessee	Date
_____	_____	_____	_____
Resident/Lessee	Date	Resident/Lessee	Date
_____	_____	_____	_____
Owner/Lessor or Owner Agent/ Lessor Agent	Date	Owner/Lessor or Owner Agent/ Lessor Agent	Date

III. Introduction to Move-In Forms

During the process of moving into a new place, a tenant will likely have a clear view of the state of the property. As the landlord, the last thing on your mind is when the tenant is moving out. But as a landlord, you will be entrusted with holding a sizable amount of money in the form of a security deposit and rent. A tenant is relying on you to be a good steward of the money.

When a tenant moves-in, you want to document the condition of the property. Better still, you want the tenant to acknowledge that you gave the property to the tenant in a certain condition. The reason is that when the tenant moves-out, you can identify the repairs that were required. This is important when the tenant is looking for the return of the security deposit. Since the security deposit is generally not used as the last month's rent, a tenant will likely be eager to get full security deposit returned. This section can help you get those documents in order.

In addition, a tenant may have questions that are better provided in writing such as the names and phone numbers for utilities. It can be time consuming looking-up every utility one-at-a-time. Your time is better served by providing this information to the tenant on their move-in. This is also good for the tenant who does not need to come to you for the information. At the same time, you can remind the tenant of the parking policy or get a referral from the tenant to get more tenants.

This section provides all of this as well as a formal repair request so your tenant can better communicate with you about the repairs that are needed. Fixing minor repairs may save from more costly repairs down the road.

The forms in this section are optional, but can help you get organized as well as better prepare your tenant so they do not need to come to you for every issue they may possibly handle.

Move-In Checklist

- ❏ Movie-In Checklist
- ❏ Welcome Letter
- ❏ Move-In Walk-Through Statement of Condition
- ❏ Move-In Walk-Through Statement of Condition Supplement for Furnished Premises
- ❏ Utilities Contact Information
- ❏ Parking Policy
- ❏ Referral Card
- ❏ Repair Request Form
- ❏ _____
- ❏ _____
- ❏ _____

Comments: _____

_____

_____

_____

_____

_____

_____

_____

_____

_____

_____

_____

_____

_____

Welcome Letter

Welcome! My goal is to make coming home the best part of your day! If I can help make that happen, please let me know. Inside this packet, you will find a variety of information to make your move easier, including the following:

- ❑ Contact Information
- ❑ Internet/TV Providers
- ❑ Move-In Walk-Through Statement of Condition
- ❑ Move-In Walk-Through Statement of Condition Supplement for Furnished Premises
- ❑ Utilities Contact Information
- ❑ Parking Policy
- ❑ Referral Card
- ❑ Tenant Repair Request

- ❑ _____
- ❑ _____
- ❑ _____
- ❑ _____
- ❑ _____
- ❑ _____

Essential Contact Information

Resident Address: _____

_____

Internet/TV Providers

Landlord Name: _____ Phone Number: _____

Address: _____

_____

Company Name: _____ Phone Number: _____

Website: _____ Note: _____

Company Name: _____ Phone Number: _____

Website: _____ Note: _____

Sincerely,

_____

Move-In Walk-Through Statement of Condition

Lease Start Date: _____   Inspection Date: _____

Premises Address: _____

_____

_____

Resident(s) Name : _____

_____

Prepared By: _____

*Unless otherwise noted, the Premises are in clean, good working order and undamaged

Area:	Move-In Condition:	Comments:
Living Room ☐ N/A		
Kitchen ☐ N/A		
Dining Room ☐ N/A		
Cabinetry ☐ N/A		
Appliances ☐ N/A		

Area:	Move-In Condition:	Comments:
Hallway ❏ N/A		
Flooring		
Light Fixtures		
Light Bulbs		
Ceiling Fans ❏ N/A ❏ Number:		
Air Conditioning ❏ N/A ❏ Central		
Heat ❏ N/A ❏ Central		
Detectors ❏ Smoke#: ❏ Carbon Monoxide #:		
Walls		
Windows		

Area:	Move-In Condition:	Comments:
Doors		
Screens		
Blinds ❑ N/A		
Closets		
Mirrors		
Outlets		
Bedroom 1 ❑ N/A		
Bedroom 2 ❑ N/A		
Bedroom 3 ❑ N/A		
Bathroom 1		
Bathroom 2 ❑ N/A		
Bathroom 3 ❑ N/A		

Area:	Move-In Condition:	Comments:
Outdoor Area ❏ N/A		
Balcony ❏ N/A		
Additional Comments:		

RESIDENT SIGNATURE: _____ DATE: _____

RESIDENT SIGNATURE: _____ DATE: _____

RESIDENT SIGNATURE: _____ DATE: _____

RESIDENT SIGNATURE: _____ DATE: _____

LANDLORD SIGNATURE: _____ DATE: _____

Move-In Walk-Through Statement of Condition Supplement for Furnished Premises

Lease Start Date: _____   Inspection Date: _____

Premises Address: _____

_____

_____

Resident(s) Name : _____

_____

Prepared By: _____

*Unless otherwise noted, the Premises are in clean, good working order and undamaged

Area:	Move-In Condition:	Comments:
Living Room		
❑ Sofa(s)		
❑ TV		
❑ TV Stand/Cabinet		
❑ Coffee Table		
❑ Light(s)		
❑ Side Table(s)		
❑ Rug		
❑ Painting(s)		
❑ _____		
❑ _____		
❑ _____		
❑ _____		
❑ _____		
❑ _____		
❑ N/A		

Area:	Move-In Condition:	Comments:
Kitchen ☐ Microwave ☐ Cookware ☐ Utensils/Plates ☐ Refrigerator(s) ☐ Toaster ☐ Table/Chairs ☐ Clock ☐ Mat(s) ☐ Painting(s) ☐ _____ ☐ _____ ☐ _____ ☐ _____ ☐ _____ ☐ N/A		
Dining Room ☐ Table/Chairs ☐ Cabinet ☐ Utensils/Plates ☐ Light(s) ☐ Side Table(s) ☐ Clock ☐ Rug ☐ Painting(s) ☐ _____ ☐ _____ ☐ _____ ☐ _____ ☐ N/A		

Area:	Move-In Condition:	Comments:
Bedroom 1 ❑ Bed ❑ Dresser(s) ❑ Nightstand(s) ❑ Light(s) ❑ Clock(s) ❑ TV ❑ TV Stand/Cabinet ❑ Rug ❑ Painting(s) ❑ _____ ❑ _____ ❑ _____ ❑ _____ ❑ _____ ❑ N/A		
Bedroom 2 ❑ Bed ❑ Dresser(s) ❑ Nightstand(s) ❑ Light(s) ❑ Clock(s) ❑ TV ❑ TV Stand/Cabinet ❑ Rug ❑ Painting(s) ❑ _____ ❑ _____ ❑ _____ ❑ _____ ❑ N/A		

Area:	Move-In Condition:	Comments:
Bedroom 3 ❑ Bed ❑ Dresser(s) ❑ Nightstand(s) ❑ Light(s) ❑ Clock(s) ❑ TV ❑ TV Stand/Cabinet ❑ Rug ❑ Painting(s) ❑ _____ ❑ _____ ❑ _____ ❑ _____ ❑ N/A		
Bathroom 1 ❑ Cabinet ❑ _____ ❑ _____ ❑ _____		
Bathroom 2 ❑ Cabinet ❑ _____ ❑ _____ ❑ _____		
Bathroom 3 ❑ Cabinet ❑ _____ ❑ _____		

Area:	Move-In Condition:	Comments:
Outdoor Area ❏ Outdoor Chairs ❏ Outdoor Table ❏ Outdoor Umbrella ❏ Swing ❏ _____ ❏ _____ ❏ _____ ❏ _____ ❏ N/A		
❏ _____ ❏ _____ ❏ _____ ❏ _____		
❏ _____ ❏ _____ ❏ _____		

Additional Comments:

RESIDENT SIGNATURE: _____ DATE: _____

RESIDENT SIGNATURE: _____ DATE: _____

RESIDENT SIGNATURE: _____ DATE: _____

RESIDENT SIGNATURE: _____ DATE: _____

LANDLORD SIGNATURE: _____ DATE: _____

Utilities Contact Information

❏ Electric: _____   Phone: _____

       Website: _____   Note: _____

❏ Water: _____   Phone: _____

       Website: _____   Note: _____

❏ Cable/Internet: _____   Phone: _____

       Website: _____   Note: _____

❏ Gas: _____   Phone: _____

       Website: _____   Note: _____

❏ Name: _____   Phone: _____

       Website: _____   Note: _____

❏ Name: _____   Phone: _____

       Website: _____   Note: _____

❏ Name: _____   Phone: _____

       Website: _____   Note: _____

❏ Name: _____   Phone: _____

       Website: _____   Note: _____

❏ Name: _____   Phone: _____

       Website: _____   Note: _____

Parking Policy

1. Parking availability is limited. Parking is assigned as follows:

   ❑ Free parking is provided for _____ number of vehicles. ❑ Additional vehicles will be provided for a monthly fee, per Parking Addendum.

   ❑ Parking is provided for a monthly fee, per Parking Addendum.

   ❑ Additional unassigned street parking is available.

2. Vehicles parked on the Premises must be registered to Resident and maintain current State vehicle registration tags. The license plate number, make, and model of the vehicle are required to be disclosed to the Owner. Also, a copy of the Resident's State-issued Driver's license will be required. All vehicles on Premises must be registered with Owner. Cars, trucks, boats, trailers, motorcycles, recreational vehicles, or commercial vehicles are prohibited on the Premises without the express prior written consent of the Owner.

3. Residents are required to keep the Owner informed of vehicle license numbers of any vehicles that will be parked on the Premises.

4. Parking permits, if provided, are to be properly displayed at all times.

5. Vehicle maintenance, upkeep, and/or repairs are **NOT** permitted on the Premises. No car parts, broken or disabled vehicles are stored on the Premises or anywhere else on the Premises. Non-operative vehicles will be towed at Resident's expense. No trailers, boats, campers, recreational vehicles, or trucks over one ton are allowed without prior written authorization. Prohibited activities include, but are not limited to, carwashes, painting, repairs of any kind, and oil changes.

6. The parking areas are not for storage. Combustible, hazardous, explosive materials, or dangerous accumulations of rubbish, wastepaper, boxes, shavings, or any highly flammable materials is not permitted as this is a fire violation and safety hazard.

7. Garage doors, if any, must be kept closed. WARNING: rain and moisture can cause a garage door to shut unexpectedly due to added weight. Please be aware of this possibility and advise the Owner if you notice any problem with the operation of any garage doors.

8. All cars are to be kept in a clean, orderly, and operative condition. Vehicles with $500.00 or more in damages as a result of an accident or otherwise, flat tires, non-operational vehicles, and vehicles left in the same spot for over 72 hours are subject to immediate tow at the expense of the vehicle owner.

9. Vehicle leaks are strictly prohibited and may be the basis for the termination of this Addendum or Lease Agreement. The Resident agrees to pay the Owner a fee of $ 100.00 for every occurrence where the Owner must, as determined at the Owner's sole discretion, clean oil or other fluids from the Premises due to any leaks from any vehicles owned or operated by the Resident, their household, guests, invitees, or agents.

10. Owner reserves the right to prohibit any vehicle on the Premises, including oversized vehicles and vehicles with altered or modified mufflers or exhaust systems whereby the noise level is judged by the Owner or its agents to constitute a nuisance or disturbance to others, or any other vehicle displaying anything potentially offensive.

11. Vehicles not registered with the Owner are in violation of this Addendum and whether legally or illegally parked, will be towed away at the Vehicle owner's expense. Parking in designated fire lanes, double parking, or parking on the grass is prohibited, and violators may be towed at the vehicle owner's expense.

Comments: _____

_____

_____

_____

_____

_____

_____

_____

_____

_____

_____

_____

_____

_____

_____

_____

Referral Card

Date: _____

Referred by current Resident (name): _____ phone: _____

This card refers new Resident (name): _____ phone: _____

to the Premises located at: _____

_____

Signature: _____

Referral Bonus: $ _____ paid on new Resident move-in to the current Resident to be applied towards monthly rent with no cash value.

Repair Request Form

Date: _____

Current Resident (name): _____ Phone: _____

Premises located at: _____

_____

Please provide a brief description of the problem(s) that need to be repaired: _____

_____

_____

_____

_____

_____

_____

_____

_____

_____

_____

_____

_____

❑ I grant permission to the Landlord, Landlord's Agents, and sub-contractor(s) under the Landlord's direction to enter Premises for the purpose of making the necessary repairs if I am not present.

Signature: _____

IV.   Introduction to Landlord Forms

Landlords can have a very difficult time. There are times where a tenant who looks great on paper is very difficult. There are also times where a tenant is an ideal tenant, and you want to extend their lease agreement. There are also times where a tenant is having checks returned or violating the lease agreement. This section can help in some of those circumstances.

As a landlord, you are expected to understand what is contained in the lease agreement. Some tenants also understand what is in a lease agreement and others will look to you as the expert. Therefore, you need more tools when tenant issues arise. This section includes tools for you to: keep track of monthly tenant rent payments, provide receipts to tenant after they pay rent, extend the lease agreement, and deal with bad tenant behavior.

While one returned check may be forgiven, multiple bounced checks can be a sign that the tenant is likely to repeat this behavior. There are also times where a tenant has violated the lease agreement too many times and you want them out. As a landlord, you should document and notify the tenant of violations to the lease agreement. As with most things in the law, documentation and notices are key to showing that you have made efforts to peacefully resolve the issue and that genuine issues have occurred in the past.

There are times where a tenant has committed multiple violations of the lease agreement and you want the tenant out but do not feel comfortable evicting a tenant. You may be willing to pay the tenant to leave. For these times, this section includes a Cash for Keys Agreement that pays the tenant to vacate peacefully. Sometimes it is simply worth paying a bad tenant to leave the property.

Fair housing laws do not allow discrimination based on certain classifications. Therefore, it is not recommended that a tenant be evicted, paid to move, or otherwise because of their race, gender, religion, etc. as that is prohibited activity.

Whether you are a professional property manager or have one property to manage, the proper forms can make the difference between success and failure. Use the forms in this section to deal with common issues landlord's face. The forms can help you communicate with tenants and protect your rights as a landlord and theirs as tenants.

Receipt of Monthly for Payment

Date Received: _____ Total Received $ _____

❑ Check ❑ Money Order Check No: _____ ❑ _____

Received from: _____

Premises Address: _____

_____

_____

Received by Landlord: _____

Address: _____

_____

_____

Authorized signature: _____

Notes: _____

_____

_____

_____

_____

_____

_____

_____

_____

_____

_____

_____

_____

_____

_____

_____

Monthly Rent Payment Record Log

Received from Tenant: _____

Address: _____

_____

_____

Rental Month:	Amount:	Date Received:	Check #:	Notes:
	$			
	$			
	$			
	$			
	$			
	$			
	$			
	$			
	$			
	$			
	$			
	$			
	$			
	$			
	$			
	$			
	$			
	$			
	$			
	$			

Increase in Monthly Tenant Rent Letter

_____

_____

_____

Date: _____

Dear Tenant(s)_____,

Please be advised that effective _____ the monthly rent for the Premises located at:

_____

_____, where

you are a Tenant, will be increased to $_____ /month payable according to the terms of the Lease Agreement. This is an increase from your previous rent. All other terms of your Lease Agreement and Addendums will remain in effect. Please sign in the space below, indicating your agreement to the new rental rate to continue your tenancy.

Tenant(s) Signature: _____   Date: _____

Tenant(s) Signature: _____   Date: _____

Tenant(s) Signature: _____   Date: _____

Tenant(s) Signature: _____   Date: _____

Feel free to contact me with any questions or concerns.

Sincerely,

Landlord Signature: _____

Printed Name: _____

Telephone: _____

Email: _____

Landlord Offer to Extend Lease Agreement

_____

_____

_____

Date: _____

Dear Tenant(s)_____,

Thank you for being a Tenant at _____

_____

under a Lease Agreement that commenced on _____.

I am writing to inform you that your current Lease Agreement will expire on _____.

You've been a great Tenant, and I would like to offer you a ❑ _____-month ❑ one-year renewal at

$_____/month.

If you are interested, I will send you an Agreement to Extend Lease. If you have any questions or concerns, I'm happy to discuss them with you.

Please let me know if you are interested by _____.

Sincerely,

Landlord Signature: _____

Printed Name: _____

Telephone: _____

Email: _____

Addendum to Extend Lease Agreement

This Addendum is entered into by and between _____,

"Owner/Agent" and _____, "Resident."

Resident is renting from Owner the "Premises" located at: _____

_____

under a Lease Agreement that commenced on _____. This Addendum is incorporated into the Lease Agreement between Lessor and Lessee, and this Addendum controls in the event of conflict with the Lease Agreement. This Addendum supersedes all oral and prior written agreements regarding extending the Lease. The Parties acknowledge that no representation, inducements, promises, or agreements have been made by or on behalf of any party, except those covenants and agreements in this written agreement. Where context requires, the singular will include the plural, the plural the singular, and genders will include all genders. All Federal, State, and local laws apply where omitted. In consideration of the mutual promises, Owner and Resident agree as follows:

1. **EXTEND LEASE.** The Owner and Resident in this Addendum agree to extend the Lease Agreement for a period of _____ months, beginning at the end of the Lease Agreement.

2. **TERMS AND CONDITIONS.** All of the terms and conditions in the original Lease Agreement and Addendums (unless provided below) will remain in full effect during the terms of this extended Lease Agreement, except:

   a. Resident agrees to pay the Owner $ _____ /month as rent due under the same terms and method as described in the Lease Agreement.

   b. All Addendums will remain in force, except: _____

Comments: _____

_____

_____

_____

_____

By signing below, Resident confirms that he/she has received, reviewed, and understands this Addendum.

_____	_____	_____	_____
Resident/Lessee	Date	Resident/Lessee	Date
_____	_____	_____	_____
Resident/Lessee	Date	Resident/Lessee	Date
_____	_____	_____	_____
Owner/Lessor or Owner Agent/ Lessor Agent	Date	Owner/Lessor or Owner Agent/ Lessor Agent	Date

Acceptance of Notice of Intent to Vacate

_____

_____

_____

Date: _____

Dear Tenant(s)_____,

Thank you for being a Tenant at _____

_____

Your notice of intent to vacate has been accepted. Accordingly, your Lease Agreement will end on

_____.   Your Security Deposit(s) may _NOT_ be used as your last month's rent. Rent is due through the end of the Lease Agreement, and rent must still be paid in advance on the normal rental date. The rent is prorated to the end of the Lease Agreement to:

From _____ to _____, (that is _____ days at

a rate of $_____ / day) equals a total prorated amount of $_____

The failure to vacate the Premises at the end of the agreed upon date will incur a charge equal to _____ times the monthly rental rate. If you move earlier than the end of the termination, and if the Landlord reassumes possession of the Premises, the Landlord will attempt to rent the Premises, but makes not promises. If the Landlord is successful in obtaining rent for a period prior to termination, you will be given credit for that time up until the termination date.

Please give all keys to the Landlord or leave them on the kitchen counter for collection. A charge will be applied if the keys are not accounted for by the termination date.

You do not need to be there when the walk-through inspection is performed. If you would like to be present, please notify us, within a reasonable time to schedule an appointment.

Any and all repairs, repainting, trash removal, cleaning, and any other expenses that are attributed to restoring the Premises to its condition prior to the tenancy will be deducted from the Security Deposit, per the Lease Agreement.

The most frequent charges for move-outs include cleaning the top and inside of the refrigerator and oven, soap scum on tub/shower, wiping cabinets/baseboards, ceiling fans and lights. Stove, microwave, refrigerator, freezer, dishwasher, exhaust fan, windows, blinds, air conditioner, light fixtures, doors, radiators, baseboards, and bathrooms must be thoroughly cleaned. DO NOT turn refrigerator off. Tile or hardwood floors must be cleaned. Before leaving your keys, please make sure the thermostat is set to "Auto" and set at 60ºF during the winter and 78ºF during the summer. Close all blinds and turn off all of the lights. Close and lock all windows. Lock all patio/balcony doors, if any. Exterior of Premises must be clean and free of debris. Additional charges may be incurred due to damage from nicotine or cooking odors e.g., smell, discoloration of blinds, walls, ceilings, cabinets.

In addition, some other frequent charges for move-out are repairs and replacements include patching and painting nail holes, burnt out light bulbs, broken blinds, and batteries for detectors. If you need touch-up paint for any holes or marks on the walls, please let us know so we may guide provide the appropriate paint colors. Please make us aware of any damage or issues within the Premises.

State law permits former tenants to reclaim abandoned personal property left at the former address of the tenant, subject to certain conditions. You may or may not be able to reclaim property without additional costs, depending on the costs of storing the property and the length of the time before it is reclaimed. In general, these costs will be lower the sooner you contact the Landlord.

Please provide the Landlord with a forwarding address as soon as possible so that there will be no delay with the return of the Security Deposit(s). Per the Lease Agreement, one (1) check will be issued with all of the Tenant names. Please allow _____ days from the Lease Agreement Termination Date for processing. Any damage beyond normal wear and tear will be charged according to the Lease Agreement.

In order to avoid missing or returned mail, be sure to complete a change of address with the U.S. Post Office here: https://moversguide.usps.com/mgo/disclaimer or by visiting the local U.S. Post Office.

Please remember to deliver the Premises in the same condition they were in prior to your arrival.

Comments: _____

_____

_____

_____

_____

_____

_____

_____

_____

Good luck with your move,

Signature: _____

Printed Name: _____

Telephone: _____

Email: _____

Advanced Notice to Enter Premises

Date: _____

Dear Tenant(s) _____,

This letter is advanced notice that the Landlord and/or its agents will access the Premises

on _____ between _____:_____ am/pm to _____:_____ am/pm to:

- ❑ Make ❑ necessary repairs/ ❑ agreed repairs
- ❑ Make necessary or agreed ❑ alterations/ ❑ improvements
- ❑ Supply necessary or agreed services
- ❑ Exhibit the rental property to prospective or actual ❑ tenants/ ❑ purchasers/ ❑ mortgagees
- ❑ Exhibit the rental property to workmen or contractors
- ❑ Pursuant to a Court Order
- ❑ Inspect prior to the termination of the Lease Agreement, as requested by the Tenant(s)
- ❑ Inspect for ❑ Pests/ ❑ Bed Bugs/ ❑ Water Damage/ ❑ Waterbed or liquid-filled furniture
- ❑ Test the ❑ smoke detector(s) and/or ❑ carbon monoxide detector(s)
- ❑ Verify that the Tenant has abandoned the Premises
- ❑ Emergency _____
- ❑ _____

Feel free to contact me with any questions or concerns.

Sincerely,

Signature: _____

Printed Name: _____

Telephone: _____

Email: _____

This Notice was delivered by: (Proof of Service Included)
❑ Certified Mail ❑ Hand Delivery to Tenant ❑ Posting in a conspicuous location at the leased Premises

Proof of Service

To be filled out by Server AFTER service on Resident is complete

I, the undersigned, being at least 18 years of age, declare that I served this notice, of which this is a true

copy, on the _____day of _____(month), _____ (year), in

_____ (city), _____ (state), on the Tenant

named in the attached notice who is in possession of the Premises in the manner indicated below.

❑ **BY DELIVERING** the notice personally to the Resident or to someone of suitable age and discretion at the premises at least 24 hours prior to the intended entry, or at least 48 hours prior to entry in the case of an initial inspection prior to terminating the tenancy as required by law.

❑ **BY LEAVING** a copy of the notice at, near, or under the usual entry door of the premises at least 24 hours prior to the intended entry in a manner in which a reasonable person would discover the notice, or at least 48 hours prior to entry in the case of an initial inspection prior to terminating the tenancy as required.

❑ **BY MAILING** a copy of the notice addressed to the Resident at least 6 days prior to intended entry.

I declare under penalty of perjury that the foregoing is true and correct and if called as a witness to testify thereto, I could do so competently.

_____   _____

(Signature of Declarant)   Date

Notice of Entry of Residence

Date: _____

Dear Tenant(s) _____,

This letter is to provide notice that the Landlord and/or its agents accessed the Premises located at:

_____

_____

on _____ between ____:_____ am/pm to ____:_____ am/pm to:

- ❑ Make ❑ necessary repairs/ ❑ agreed repairs

- ❑ Make necessary or agreed ❑ alterations/ ❑ improvements

- ❑ Supply necessary or agreed services

- ❑ Exhibit the rental property to prospective or actual ❑ tenants/ ❑ purchasers/ ❑ mortgagees

- ❑ Exhibit the rental property to workmen or contractors

- ❑ Pursuant to a Court Order

- ❑ Inspect prior to the termination of the Lease Agreement, as requested by the Tenant(s)

- ❑ Inspect for ❑ Pests/ ❑ Bed Bugs/ ❑ Water Damage/ ❑ Waterbed or liquid-filled furniture

- ❑ Test the ❑ smoke detector(s) and/or ❑ carbon monoxide detector(s)

- ❑ Verify that the Tenant has abandoned the Premises

- ❑ Emergency _____

- ❑ _____

Feel free to contact me with any questions or concerns.

Signature: _____

Printed Name: _____

Telephone: _____

Email: _____

This Notice was delivered by: (Proof of Service Included)
❑ Certified Mail ❑ Hand Delivery to Tenant ❑ Posting in a conspicuous location at the leased Premises

Proof of Service

To be filled out by Server AFTER service on Resident is complete

I, the undersigned, being at least 18 years of age, declare that I served this notice, of which this is a true copy, on the _____ day of _____ (month), _____ (year), in _____ (city), _____ (state), on the Tenant named in the attached notice who is in possession of the Premises in the manner indicated below.

❏ **BY DELIVERING** the notice personally to the Resident or to someone of suitable age and discretion at the premises at least 24 hours prior to the intended entry, or at least 48 hours prior to entry in the case of an initial inspection prior to terminating the tenancy as required by law.

❏ **BY LEAVING** a copy of the notice at, near, or under the usual entry door of the premises at least 24 hours prior to the intended entry in a manner in which a reasonable person would discover the notice, or at least 48 hours prior to entry in the case of an initial inspection prior to terminating the tenancy as required.

❏ **BY MAILING** a copy of the notice addressed to the Resident at least 6 days prior to intended entry.

I declare under penalty of perjury that the foregoing is true and correct and if called as a witness to testify thereto, I could do so competently.

_____   _____

(Signature of Declarant)   Date

Notice of Violation

_____

_____

_____

Date: _____

Dear Tenant(s)_____,

This letter is a formal Notice that you are in violation of the terms of the Lease Agreement for the Premises you are renting located at _____

_____

The violation(s) are as follows: _____

_____

_____

_____

_____

_____

_____

Per State law, you have _____ calendar days to cure this violation, as it is materially affecting health and safety. If you fail to cure this violation within these days, the Lease Agreement may be subject to termination. **Please sign below and send back this Notice as an indication that you have received it.** You may respond to this Notice of Violation in writing. Feel free to contact me with any questions or concerns.

Sincerely,

Signature: _____

Printed Name: _____

Telephone: _____

Email: _____

Cash for Keys Agreement

This Cash for Keys Agreement is entered into by and between:_____

"Owner/Agent" and _____, "Resident."

Resident is renting from Owner the "Premises" located at: _____

_____

_____

All state, and local laws apply if omitted. In consideration of the mutual promises, Owner and Resident agree as follows:

1. **AGREEMENT TO VACATE/RELOCATION ASSISTANCE.** Resident covenants and agrees to voluntarily vacate the Premises by _____ am/pm on _____ In exchange for the timely, peaceful surrender of possession of the Premises by Resident, Owner agrees to pay Resident the sum of $_____ ("Relocation Assistance"). The sum will increase or decrease by $ _____ / day. It will increase for each day the Resident moves out that is earlier than the stated move-out date; and it will decrease by the same amount for each extra day Resident takes to vacate beyond the stated move-out date.

2. **INSPECTION AND CONDITION OF THE PREMISES.** Within 24 hours of Resident's move-out, Resident will make a final inspection of the Premises. If Resident has vacated the Premises by the move-out date, returned all keys, and has left the Premises (including all fixtures, facilities, and appliances) in the same condition as they were on move-in, ordinary wear and tear excepted, Resident will immediately pay Resident the full amount of the Relocation Assistance by check.

3. **LIABILITY FOR PERSONAL OR REAL PROPERTY DAMAGE.** Resident will not deliberately or negligently destroy, deface, damage, impair, or remove any part of the Premises (including fixtures, facilities, and appliances) or permit any persons to do so whether known by the Resident or not, and Resident will be responsible for any damage caused by his failure to comply with this requirement. All persons and personal property in or on the Premises will be at the sole risk and responsibility of Resident. Owner will not be liable for any injury or damage whatsoever to the person or property of Resident or any person or entity in or on the Premises; and Resident expressly agrees to indemnify and hold Owner harmless in all such matters.

4. **DEFAULT.** In the event Owner determines that damage to the Premises has occurred, which was caused by the willful acts, acts of omission, or the negligence, Owner will deduct cost of repairs from the Relocation Assistance. In the event the costs of the repairs exceed the amount of the Relocation Assistance, Resident will be personally liable for all repair costs which exceed the amount of the Relocation Assistance. Owner will also be entitled to avail itself of all other rights and remedies to which it may be entitled, either at law or equity and Owner will be entitled to recover any reasonable attorney's fees and any other costs provided by law. In the even Resident fails to vacate the Premises prior to the expiration of the term of the Agreement, Resident forfeits any right to receive the Relocation Assistance or any portion

thereof and Owner will commence eviction proceedings against Resident. Owner will be entitled to recover reasonable attorney's fees, eviction expenses, court costs, and any other costs provided by law.

5. **PRIOR LEASE AGREEMENT.** If Resident is currently in possession of the Premises as a result of a Lease Agreement between Owner and Resident, Resident agrees to continue to be bound during the term of this Agreement by all conditions, restrictions, and covenants contained in the Lease Agreement. Any default under the terms of the Lease Agreement will also be a violation of this Agreement. In the event there is a conflict between the provisions set forth in the Lease Agreement and this Agreement, the provisions of this Agreement will prevail.

6. **SEVERABILITY/UNENFORCEABILITY.** All individual provisions, paragraphs, sentences, clauses, sections, and words in this Agreement will be severable and if any one or more such parts are determined by a court, administrative body, or tribunal, having proper jurisdiction, to be unenforceable, or to be in any way violative of or in conflict with any law of any applicable jurisdiction, such determination will have no effect on any of the remaining parts of this Agreement that remain.

7. **ENTIRE AGREEMENT.** This Agreement supersedes any oral or prior written agreements between the Owner and Resident, including the Lease Agreement. The Owner and Resident acknowledge that no representation, inducements, promises, or agreements have been made by or on behalf of any party, except those covenants and agreements in this written Agreement. All covenants are to be construed as conditions of this Agreement. Where context requires, the singular will include the plural, the plural the singular, and genders will include all genders.

Comments: _____

_____

_____

_____

_____

_____

_____

_____

_____

By signing below, Resident confirms that he/she has received, reviewed, and understands this Agreement.

Resident/Lessee	Date	Resident/Lessee	Date
Resident/Lessee	Date	Resident/Lessee	Date
Owner/Lessor or Owner Agent/ Lessor Agent	Date	Owner/Lessor or Owner Agent/ Lessor Agent	Date

Rental Termination Notice

_____

_____

_____

Date: _____

RE: TERMINATION

Dear Tenant(s)_____,

This is formal Notice that the Lease Agreement for the Premises that you are renting located at

_____

_____

will terminate on _____.

According to the Lease Agreement, you are hereby notified and required to vacate the Premises on or before the termination date.

Feel free to contact me with any questions or concerns.

    Sincerely,

    Signature: _____

    Printed Name: _____

    Telephone: _____

    Email: _____

This Notice was delivered by: (Proof of Service Included)
❑ Certified Mail ❑ Hand Delivery to Tenant ❑ Posting in a conspicuous location at the leased Premises

Proof of Service

To be filled out by Server AFTER service on Resident is complete

I, the undersigned, being at least 18 years of age, declare that I served this notice, of which this is a true copy, on the _____ day of _____ (month), _____ (year), in _____ (city), _____ (state), on the Tenant named in the attached notice who is in possession of the Premises in the manner indicated below.

❑ **BY DELIVERING** the notice personally to the Resident or to someone of suitable age and discretion at the premises at least 24 hours prior to the intended entry, or at least 48 hours prior to entry in the case of an initial inspection prior to terminating the tenancy as required by law.

❑ **BY LEAVING** a copy of the notice at, near, or under the usual entry door of the premises at least 24 hours prior to the intended entry in a manner in which a reasonable person would discover the notice, or at least 48 hours prior to entry in the case of an initial inspection prior to terminating the tenancy as required.

❑ **BY MAILING** a copy of the notice addressed to the Resident at least 6 days prior to intended entry.

I declare under penalty of perjury that the foregoing is true and correct and if called as a witness to testify thereto, I could do so competently.

_____   _____

(Signature of Declarant)   Date

Notice to Vacate

_____

_____

_____

Date: _____

RE: VACATE

Dear Tenant(s)_____,

This is formal Notice that you vacate the Premises that you currently occupy located at:

_____

_____

❑ This is a ____-Day Notice due to your <u>delinquency to pay rent</u> on the Premises. If you do not comply with this Notice within _____ days of the Certificate of Service, I will be forced to proceed to obtain possession of the Premises and have you removed by law.

❑ This is a ____-Day Notice due to your breach of the Lease Agreement. If you do not comply with this Notice within _____ days of the Certificate of Service, I will be forced to proceed to obtain possession of the Premises and have you removed by law.

Sincerely,

Signature: _____

Printed Name: _____

Telephone: _____

Email: _____

This Notice was delivered by: (Proof of Service Included)
❑ Certified Mail ❑ Hand Delivery to Tenant ❑ Posting in a conspicuous location at the leased Premises

Proof of Service

To be filled out by Server AFTER service on Resident is complete

I, the undersigned, being at least 18 years of age, declare that I served this notice, of which this is a true copy, on the _____ day of _____(month), _____ (year), in _____ (city), _____ (state), on the Tenant named in the attached notice who is in possession of the Premises in the manner indicated below.

❏ **BY DELIVERING** the notice personally to the Resident or to someone of suitable age and discretion at the premises at least 24 hours prior to the intended entry, or at least 48 hours prior to entry in the case of an initial inspection prior to terminating the tenancy as required by law.

❏ **BY LEAVING** a copy of the notice at, near, or under the usual entry door of the premises at least 24 hours prior to the intended entry in a manner in which a reasonable person would discover the notice, or at least 48 hours prior to entry in the case of an initial inspection prior to terminating the tenancy as required.

❏ **BY MAILING** a copy of the notice addressed to the Resident at least 6 days prior to intended entry.

I declare under penalty of perjury that the foregoing is true and correct and if called as a witness to testify thereto, I could do so competently.

_____   _____

(Signature of Declarant)   Date

Demand to Make Good on Bad Check

_____

_____

_____

Date: _____

RE: DEMAND LETTER

Dear Tenant(s)_____,

The rent check you wrote on: _____ (check #: _____), was

returned by the bank due to ❑ account was closed OR ❑ the account had insufficient funds.

Unless full payment of the check amount is received within _____ calendar days from the date of

this letter, along with bank fees that were required to process the bad check, and the cost of mailing this letter by Certified Mail, a small claims court claim will be filed against you.

The total amount due is: $ _____.

The small claims court will be filed in state court and will claim 1) the full amount of bad check, 2) bank

fees, 3) the cost of mailing this Demand Letter by Certified Mail, 4) and damages assessed at three times the amount of the check (calculated by starting with a minimum penalty of $100 up to a maximum penalty of $1,500, under State Civil Code).

You may wish to contact a lawyer to discuss your legal rights and responsibilities.

Please send your payment to: _____

_____

_____

Sincerely,

Signature: _____

Printed Name: _____

Telephone: _____

Email: _____

Agreement for Delayed Rent Payment

This Agreement is entered into by and between _____,

"Owner/Agent" and _____ , "Resident."

Resident is renting from Owner the "Premises" located at: _____

_____

under a Lease Agreement that commenced on _____.

This Agreement supersedes any oral or prior written agreement regarding delaying rent payment. The Parties acknowledge that no representation, inducements, promises, or agreements have been made by or on behalf of any party, except those covenants and agreements in this written agreement. Where context requires, the singular will include the plural, the plural the singular, and genders will include all genders. All Federal, State, and local laws apply where omitted. In consideration of the mutual promises, Owner and Resident agree as follows:

Resident has made a rental payment of $_____ on _____

which does **NOT** cover the full monthly rent. The partial payment is hereby accepted by Owner, leaving the remaining balance of $_____ which is delinquent and still due. The Owner agrees to accept the delinquent balance on or before _____. Owner agrees to delay any legal proceedings to evict, accrue fees, or otherwise until agreed.

Resident agrees that the Owner may continue with an eviction and legal proceedings in the event the balance of the rent is not paid by the agreed date. Owner does not waive the right to proceed with an eviction by acceptance of this payment or entering into this Agreement.

Comments: _____

_____

_____

_____

_____

_____

_____

By signing below, Resident confirms that he/she has received, reviewed, and understands this Agreement.

_____	_____	_____	_____
Resident/Lessee	Date	Resident/Lessee	Date
_____	_____	_____	_____
Resident/Lessee	Date	Resident/Lessee	Date
_____	_____	_____	_____
Owner/Lessor or Owner Agent/ Lessor Agent	Date	Owner/Lessor or Owner Agent/ Lessor Agent	Date

Agreement for Partial Rent Payment

This Agreement is entered into by and between _____,

"Owner/Agent" and _____, "Resident."

Resident is renting from Owner the "Premises" located at: _____

_____

under a Lease Agreement that commenced on _____.

This Agreement supersedes any oral or prior written agreement regarding a partial rent payment. The Parties acknowledge that no representation, inducements, promises, or agreements have been made by or on behalf of any party, except those covenants and agreements in this written agreement. Where context requires, the singular will include the plural, the plural the singular, and genders will include all genders. All Federal, State, and local laws apply where omitted.

Resident has made a rental payment of $_____ on _____

which does **NOT** cover the full monthly rent. The partial payment is hereby accepted by Owner, leaving the remaining balance of $_____ which is delinquent and still due.

In consideration of the mutual promises, Owner and Resident agree as follows:

1. **NO RIGHTS WAIVED**. Partial payment is accepted by the Owner based on the promises that Owner does not waive any legal rights, including the right to collect the full amount due, late charges, interest, and the right to bring an action for possession of the rental unit. This Agreement is for the benefit of the Tenant(s).

2. **NO TIME-RELATED WAIVERS**. Acceptance of the partial payment does not impact a waiver (express or implied) of time related provision of the Lease Agreement. The partial payment will be applied as follows: first, to legal fees and court costs, then to accrued interest on amounts owed to the Owner, then to late fees, then to amounts owed for damages to the Premises, then to any other amounts owed to Owner, then to unpaid past due rent, and finally to prepaid rent. The balance due must be paid by _____.

3. **DEFAULT**. In the event of Resident default, Owner may proceed with legal action to recover past rent, damages, possession of the leased Premises, and any other relief permissible by law and the Lease Agreement.

4. **NO RESTART OF TIME**. If previously served with a Notice to Pay or Quit, acceptance by the Owner of a partial payment will not restart the time running for compliance. Owner agrees to delay any legal proceedings to evict, accrue additional fees, or otherwise until the date agreed to in this Agreement.

5. **LEAVE ACTIONS**. Resident agrees that Owner may continue with an eviction and legal proceedings in the event the balance of the rent is not paid by the agreed date. Owner does not waive the right to proceed with an eviction by the acceptance of this partial payment or entering into this Agreement.

Comments: _____

_____

_____

_____

_____

_____

_____

By signing below, Resident confirms that he/she has received, reviewed, and understands this Agreement.

_____	_____	_____	_____
Resident/Lessee	Date	Resident/Lessee	Date
_____	_____	_____	_____
Resident/Lessee	Date	Resident/Lessee	Date
_____	_____	_____	_____
Owner/Lessor or Owner Agent/ Lessor Agent	Date	Owner/Lessor or Owner Agent/ Lessor Agent	Date

Late Rent Notice

_____

_____

_____

Date: _____

RE: LATE RENT

Dear Tenant(s)_____,

This Notice is regarding late rent payment, which is a violation of the terms of the Lease Agreement for the Premises located at:_____

_____

The full rent payment has not been received as of the date of this Notice.

Rent was due on _____. You currently owe rent plus late payment

charges per the Lease Agreement. The total amount due is: $ _____.

Comments: _____

_____

_____

_____

_____

_____

If this is an oversight, please send the rent payment immediately in order to avoid incurring additional late fees. Thank you for your prompt attention to this matter. Feel free to contact me with any questions or concerns.

Sincerely,

Signature: _____

Printed Name: _____

Telephone: _____

Email: _____

Final Notice of Failure to Pay Rent Prior to Legal Action

_____

_____

_____

Date: _____

RE: FINAL NOTICE

Dear Tenant(s)_____,

This Notice is regarding late rent payment, which is a violation of the terms of the Lease Agreement for the Premises located at:_____

_____

Rent has not been received in a timely manner. Continued failure to pay rent or arrange for a payment plan (if eligible) may cause legal action to reclaim possession of the rental Premises. Contact us immediately to arrange for a payment. Failure to comply with rent payment will result in a "Notice to Pay Rent or Quit," which will lead to immediate legal action to terminate the tenancy.

Comments: _____

_____

_____

_____

_____

_____

If this is an oversight, please send the rent payment immediately in order to avoid incurring additional late fees. Thank you for your prompt attention to this matter. Feel free to contact me with any questions or concerns.

    Sincerely,

    Signature: _____

    Printed Name: _____

    Telephone: _____

    Email: _____

Notice to Pay Rent or Quit

To: _____ and all other persons and occupants renting at _____

_____

_____

"Premises" that commenced on _____.

YOU ARE HEREBY NOTIFIED that rent payment is now past due and payable on the Premises. Your account is delinquent in the amount of $_____ beginning on:

_____ through_____.

YOU ARE HEREBY required to pay the rent in full plus fees within three (3) calendar days or remove and deliver possession of the Premises, or legal proceedings will be instituted against you to recover possession of the Premises, to declare forfeiture of the Lease Agreement under which you occupy the Premises, and to recover rents and damages together with court costs and attorney's fees.

AS REQUIRED by law, you are hereby notified that a negative credit report reflecting on your credit history may be submitted to a credit reporting agency if you fail to fulfill the terms of your credit obligations.

PAYMENTS must be made to Owner at the following address: _____

_____

PAYMENTS MADE IN PERSON may be delivered to Owner between the hours of 9:00 AM and 5:00 PM, Monday through Friday.

THIS NOTICE COMPLIES with City Administrative Code in that the Tenant has failed to pay rent due which the Owner is lawfully entitled under the Lease Agreement between the Tenants and Owner.

YOU ARE FURTHER NOTIFIED THAT Owner hereby elects to declare forfeiture of the Lease Agreement under which you hold possession of the Premises. Failure to perform or comply, Owner will institute legal proceedings to recover rent and possession of the Premises, which may result in a judgment against you, including costs and necessary disbursements together with possible statutory damages as provided by law for such unlawful detention.

Comments: _____

_____

Signature: _____

Printed Name: _____

Telephone: _____

Email: _____

This Notice was delivered by: (Proof of Service Included)

❏ Certified Mail ❏ Hand Delivery to Tenant ❏ Posting in a conspicuous location at the leased Premises

Certificate of Service

To be filled out by Server AFTER service on Resident is complete

I, the undersigned, being at least 18 years of age, declare that I served this notice, of which this is a true copy, on the _____ day of _____ (month), _____ (year), in _____ (city), _____ (state), on the Tenant named in the attached notice who is in possession of the Premises in the manner indicated below.

❑ **BY DELIVERING** the notice personally to the Resident or to someone of suitable age and discretion at the premises at least 24 hours prior to the intended entry, or at least 48 hours prior to entry in the case of an initial inspection prior to terminating the tenancy as required by law.

❑ **BY LEAVING** a copy of the notice at, near, or under the usual entry door of the premises at least 24 hours prior to the intended entry in a manner in which a reasonable person would discover the notice, or at least 48 hours prior to entry in the case of an initial inspection prior to terminating the tenancy as required.

❑ **BY MAILING** a copy of the notice addressed to the Resident at least 6 days prior to intended entry.

I declare under penalty of perjury that the foregoing is true and correct and if called as a witness to testify thereto, I could do so competently.

_____   _____

(Signature of Declarant)   Date

V.   Introduction to Move-Out Forms

When a tenant moves-out of a property, you as the landlord need to get the keys back from the tenant, make repairs and upgrade (as needed), prepare the property for future tenants, and complete your obligations for the tenant that just vacated the property. Part of your final duties as landlord include repairing the property from damages caused by the previous tenant and deducting costs from the security deposit of the former tenant. You will need to provide an itemization of the deductions and then return the balance of the security deposit to the tenant. This section provides you with tools to hopefully help the tenant move-out peacefully and fairly. This section includes an itemization worksheet, a walk-though statement of condition, and letters to send to the former tenant to return the security deposit.

Many tenants expect a full return of the security deposit. Security deposit disputes are a common issue between landlords and tenants and may color how the tenant feels about your property. If the tenant understands the procedures for move-out, including the condition they are supposed to leave the property when they vacate, it may likely minimize tenant issues. You want to document the condition of the property at the time the tenant moves-out. You also want to

compare the move-out forms with the move-in forms to better document the condition of the property. That way, if there are deductions to the security deposit, you will have documentation of the changes in condition. This section can help you get those documents in order.

In addition, you will need to communicate with the former tenant to return their security deposit. This section provides sample letters to help you communicate effectively and clearly.

The forms in this section are optional, but can help you get organized.

Move-Out Checklist

Date: _____

- ❑ Move-Out Checklist
- ❑ Move-Out Letter
- ❑ Checklist of Things to Do Before Moving-Out
- ❑ Move-Out Walk-Through Statement of Condition
- ❑ Move-Out Walk-Through Statement of Condition Supplement for Furnished Premises
- ❑ _____
- ❑ _____
- ❑ _____
- ❑ _____
- ❑ _____
- ❑ _____
- ❑ _____
- ❑ _____
- ❑ _____
- ❑ _____
- ❑ _____
- ❑ _____

Comments: _____

_____

_____

_____

_____

_____

_____

_____

_____

_____

_____

_____

Move-Out Letter

_____

_____

_____

Date: _____

RE: MOVE-OUT LETTER

Dear Tenant(s)_____,

Thank you for being our Tenant. As you begin the processing of moving out, I am sending this letter to help you with your transition and finalize your stay. **Please remember that your Security Deposit may _NOT_ be used as your last month's rent so be sure to pay your last month's rent on time.**

*Failure to vacate by the move-out date may incur a charge of _____ times the Monthly Rent

If you move earlier than the end of the termination, and if Owner reassumes possession of the Premises, Owner will try to rent the Premises. If Owner is successful in obtaining rent for a period prior to termination, you will be given credit for that time up until your termination date.

Please leave all keys on the kitchen counter for collection. A charge will be applied if the keys are not accounted for by the lease ending date.

You do not need to be there when the walk-through inspection is performed. If you would like to be present, please notify us, within a reasonable time to schedule an appointment.

Any and all repairs, repainting, trash removal, cleaning, and any other expenses that are attributed to restoring the Premises to its condition prior to the tenancy will be deducted from the Security Deposit, per the Lease Agreement.

The most frequent charges for move-outs include cleaning the top and inside of the refrigerator and oven, soap scum on tub/shower, wiping cabinets/baseboards, ceiling fans and lights. Stove, microwave, refrigerator, freezer, dishwasher, exhaust fan, windows, blinds, air conditioner, light fixtures, doors, radiators, baseboards, and bathrooms must be thoroughly cleaned. DO NOT turn refrigerator off. Tile or hardwood floors must be cleaned. Before leaving your keys, please make sure the thermostat is set to "Auto" and set at 60ºF during the winter and 78ºF during the summer. Close all blinds and turn off all of the lights. Close and lock all windows. Lock all patio/balcony doors, if any. Exterior of Premises must be clean and free of debris. Additional charges may be incurred due to damage from nicotine or cooking odors e.g., smell, discoloration of blinds, walls, ceilings, cabinets.

In addition, some other frequent charges for move-out are repairs and replacements include patching and painting nail holes, burnt out light bulbs, broken blinds, and batteries for detectors. If you need touch-up paint for any holes or marks on the walls, please let us know so we may guide provide the appropriate paint colors. Please make us aware of any damage or issues within the Premises.

State law permits former tenants to reclaim abandoned personal property left at the former address of the tenant, subject to certain conditions. You may or may not be able to reclaim property without additional costs, depending on the costs of storing the property and the length of the time before it is reclaimed. In general, these costs will be lower the sooner you contact the Landlord.

Please provide the Landlord with a forwarding address as soon as possible so that there will be no delay with the return of the Security Deposit(s). Per the Lease Agreement, one (1) check will be issued with all of the Tenant names. Please allow _____ days from the Lease Agreement Termination Date for processing. Any damage beyond normal wear and tear will be charged according to the Lease Agreement.

In order to avoid missing or returned mail, be sure to complete a change of address with the U.S. Post Office here: https://moversguide.usps.com/mgo/disclaimer or by visiting the local U.S. Post Office.

Please remember to deliver the Premises in the same condition they were in prior to your arrival.

Comments: _____

_____

_____

_____

_____

_____

_____

_____

_____

_____

_____

_____

_____

_____

Good luck with your move,

Signature: _____

Printed Name: _____

Telephone: _____

Email: _____

Move-Out Checklist

RETURN: ❑ Premises Key(s)   ❑ Mailbox Key(s)   ❑ _____

❑ _____   ❑ _____   ❑ _____

DISCONNECT: ❑ Gas   ❑ Electricity   ❑ Water   ❑ Sewer

❑ Trash   ❑ Heat   ❑ Hot Water   ❑ Internet/WiFi

❑ _____   ❑ _____   ❑ _____

PROVIDE: ❑ Forwarding Address

❑ Move-Out Walk-Through Statement of Condition

❑ Move-Out Walk-Through Statement of Condition Supplement for Furnished Premises

❑ _____

❑ _____

CLEAN: Living Room: ❑ Floors/Carpet(s)   ❑ Blinds   ❑ Windows   ❑ Celling Fan(s)

❑ Lights   ❑ _____   ❑ _____

Kitchen: ❑ Floor   ❑ Blinds   ❑ Windows   ❑ Celling Fan   ❑ Lights
❑ Stove/Oven   ❑ Microwave   ❑ Dishwasher   ❑ Refrigerator   ❑ Trash

❑ Sink   ❑ Cabinets   ❑ Counters   ❑ _____

❑ _____   ❑ _____   ❑ _____

Bedroom(s):   ❑ Floor   ❑ Blinds   ❑ Windows   ❑ Celling Fan   ❑ Lights
❑ _____   ❑ _____   ❑ _____

Bathroom(s):   ❑ Floor   ❑ Blinds   ❑ Windows   ❑ Lights   ❑ Trash
❑ Sink   ❑ Toilet   ❑ Tub/Shower   ❑ Cabinet   ❑ Mirrors

❑ _____   ❑ _____   ❑ _____

Outdoor Area: ❑ _____   ❑ _____   ❑ _____

Other: ❑ _____   ❑ _____   ❑ _____

❑ _____

❑ _____

❑ _____

Comments: _____

_____

_____

_____

_____

Move-Out Walk-Through Statement of Condition

Lease Start Date: _____   Inspection Date: _____

Premises Address: _____

_____

_____

Resident(s) Name : _____

_____

Prepared By: _____

*Unless otherwise noted, the Premises are in clean, good working order and undamaged

Area:	Move-Out Condition:	Comments:
Living Room ❑ N/A		
Kitchen ❑ N/A		
Dining Room ❑ N/A		
Cabinetry ❑ N/A		
Appliances ❑ N/A		

Area:	Move-Out Condition:	Comments:
Hallway ❑ N/A		
Flooring		
Light Fixtures		
Light Bulbs		
Ceiling Fans ❑ N/A ❑ Number:		
Air Conditioning ❑ N/A ❑ Central		
Heat ❑ N/A ❑ Central		
Detectors ❑ Smoke#: ❑ Carbon Monoxide #:		
Walls		
Windows		

Area:	Move-Out Condition:	Comments:
Doors		
Screens		
Blinds ❑ N/A		
Closets		
Mirrors		
Outlets		
Bedroom 1 ❑ N/A		
Bedroom 2 ❑ N/A		
Bedroom 3 ❑ N/A		
Bathroom 1		
Bathroom 2 ❑ N/A		
Bathroom 3 ❑ N/A		

Area:	Move-Out Condition:	Comments:
Outdoor Area ❏ N/A		
Balcony ❏ N/A		

Additional Comments:

RESIDENT SIGNATURE: _____ DATE: _____

RESIDENT SIGNATURE: _____ DATE: _____

RESIDENT SIGNATURE: _____ DATE: _____

RESIDENT SIGNATURE: _____ DATE: _____

LANDLORD SIGNATURE: _____ DATE: _____

Move-Out Walk-Through Statement of Condition Supplement for Furnished Premises

Lease Start Date: _____   Inspection Date: _____

Premises Address: _____

_____

_____

Resident(s) Name : _____

_____

Prepared By: _____

*Unless otherwise noted, the Premises are in clean, good working order and undamaged

Area:	Move-Out Condition:	Comments:
Living Room		
❑ Sofa(s)		
❑ TV		
❑ TV Stand/Cabinet		
❑ Coffee Table		
❑ Light(s)		
❑ Side Table(s)		
❑ Rug		
❑ Painting(s)		
❑ _____		
❑ _____		
❑ _____		
❑ _____		
❑ _____		
❑ _____		
❑ N/A		

Area:	Move-Out Condition:	Comments:
Kitchen ❑ Microwave ❑ Cookware ❑ Utensils/Plates ❑ Refrigerator(s) ❑ Toaster ❑ Table/Chairs ❑ Clock ❑ Mat(s) ❑ Painting(s) ❑ _____ ❑ _____ ❑ _____ ❑ _____ ❑ _____ ❑ N/A		
Dining Room ❑ Table/Chairs ❑ Cabinet ❑ Utensils/Plates ❑ Light(s) ❑ Side Table(s) ❑ Clock ❑ Rug ❑ Painting(s) ❑ _____ ❑ _____ ❑ _____ ❑ _____ ❑ N/A		

Area:	Move-Out Condition:	Comments:
Bedroom 1 ❑ Bed ❑ Dresser(s) ❑ Nightstand(s) ❑ Light(s) ❑ Clock(s) ❑ TV ❑ TV Stand/Cabinet ❑ Rug ❑ Painting(s) ❑ _____ ❑ _____ ❑ _____ ❑ _____ ❑ _____		
Bedroom 2 ❑ Bed ❑ Dresser(s) ❑ Nightstand(s) ❑ Light(s) ❑ Clock(s) ❑ TV ❑ TV Stand/Cabinet ❑ Rug ❑ Painting(s) ❑ _____ ❑ _____ ❑ _____ ❑ _____ ❑ N/A		

Area:	Move-Out Condition:	Comments:
Bedroom 3 ❑ Bed ❑ Dresser(s) ❑ Nightstand(s) ❑ Light(s) ❑ Clock(s) ❑ TV ❑ TV Stand/Cabinet ❑ Rug ❑ Painting(s) ❑ _____ ❑ _____ ❑ _____ ❑ _____ ❑ N/A		
Bathroom 1 ❑ Cabinet ❑ _____ ❑ _____ ❑ _____		
Bathroom 2 ❑ Cabinet ❑ _____ ❑ _____ ❑ _____		
Bathroom 3 ❑ Cabinet ❑ _____ ❑ _____		

Area:	Move-Out Condition:	Comments:
Outdoor Area ❑ Outdoor Chairs ❑ Outdoor Table ❑ Outdoor Umbrella ❑ Swing ❑ _____ ❑ _____ ❑ _____ ❑ _____ ❑ N/A		
❑ _____ ❑ _____ ❑ _____ ❑ _____		
❑ _____ ❑ _____ ❑ _____		

Additional Comments:

RESIDENT SIGNATURE: _____ DATE: _____

RESIDENT SIGNATURE: _____ DATE: _____

RESIDENT SIGNATURE: _____ DATE: _____

RESIDENT SIGNATURE: _____ DATE: _____

LANDLORD SIGNATURE: _____ DATE: _____

Move-Out Inspection Letter

_____

_____

_____

Date: _____

RE: MOVE-OUT INSPECTION

Dear Tenant(s)_____,

Thank you for being a Tenant at Premises located at _____

_____

An inspection of the Premises was conducted on: _____. The inspection was completed with the ❑ Move-In Walk-Through Statement of Condition and/or ❑ Move-Out Walk-Through Statement of Condition, in-hand, that was completed when you moved-in. An itemized security deposit statement will be issued after _____ days from the date your Lease Agreement ended. The following was found to be at issue:

    ❑   No issues were found.

    ❑   Repairs _____

    ❑   Trash Removal _____

    ❑   Cleaning _____

    ❑   _____

    ❑   _____

    ❑   _____

    ❑   _____

Comments: _____

_____

_____

_____

Be sure to provide us with a change of address and to change your address with the U.S. Post Office.

    Sincerely,

    Signature: _____

Letter of Security Deposit Return

_____

_____

_____

Date: _____

Dear Tenant(s)_____,

Thank you for being a Tenant at Premises located at _____

_____

Security Deposit Settlement	
Security Deposit:	$_____
Pet Security Deposit:	$_____
Other Security Deposit(s):	$_____
Deposit interest: @ _____%,	$_____
TOTAL DEPOSIT(S):	$_____
Unpaid rent due: from: _____ to _____:	$_____
Late Fee(s):	$_____
Cleaning:	$_____
Carpet cleaning:	$_____
Painting:	$_____
Missing Fixtures:	$_____
Damage: _____	$_____
See Itemized Security Deposit Deductions:	$_____
TOTAL CHARGES:	$_____
BALANCE DUE: OWNER:	$_____
BALANCE DUE: RESIDENT:	$_____

Signature: _____

Printed Name: _____

Telephone: _____

Email: _____

Itemized Security Deposit Deductions

Date: _____

Tenant(s) (Names): _____

Premises Rented (Address): _____

_____

Security Deposit:	$ _____
Pet Security Deposit:	$ _____
Other Security Deposit(s):	$ _____
Deposit interest: @ _____%,	$ _____
TOTAL DEPOSIT(S):	$ _____
Unpaid rent due: from: _____ to _____:	$ _____
Late Fee(s):	$ _____
Cleaning:	$ _____
Carpet cleaning:	$ _____
Painting:	$ _____
Missing Fixtures:	$ _____
Damage: _____	$ _____
Other Deductions: _____	$ _____
Other Deductions: _____	$ _____
Other Deductions: _____	$ _____
Other Deductions: _____	$ _____
Other Deductions: _____	$ _____
TOTAL CHARGES:	$ _____
BALANCE DUE: OWNER:	$ _____
BALANCE DUE: RESIDENT:	$ _____

Signature: _____

Printed Name: _____

IV. Introduction to Landlord Forms

Most tenants want the same thing landlords want: quiet enjoyment of their rental. Another words, most tenants want to pay their rent and be left alone to live their life without interference from the landlord. Most landlords are equally looking for tenants who want nothing more from the landlord than to accept the rent and leave them to live their life.

However, part of your duties as landlord include dealing with tenant issues. For example, a tenant transferring their lease and legal obligations onto someone else. Depending on how a lease agreement is structured, and your willingness to permit certain activities, a tenant may transfer his/her obligations in part or in full. In addition, a tenant may want roommates, add persons to an existing lease agreement, assign tenant's rights under a lease agreement, or sublease the property. You may or may not allow such activities. A landlord may find advantages to assignment or subleasing a lease agreement because the new tenant may have a better credit score.

This section also provides forms tenants may use to meet their needs. There are forms for tenants to provide formal notices to a landlord who is not making repairs or is failing to provide timely return of a security deposit.

These forms can help the tenant as well as better inform a landlord who receives a similar form from their tenant.

Whether you are the tenant or landlord, the proper forms can make the difference between success and failure. Use the forms in this section to deal with common issues tenant's face. The forms can help improve communications between the landlord and tenant while protecting the rights of both parties.

Apartment Hunting Worksheet

	Property:	Property:	Property:
Address			
Contact Name			
Phone #			
Other			
Rental Rate	$		
Application Fees	$		
Security Deposit	$		
Additional Deposit(s)			
Pet Fee(s)			
# of Rooms			
# of Bathrooms			
Sq. Ft.			
Countertop Type			
Flooring Type			
Patio	❑ Yes; ❑ No	❑ Yes; ❑ No	❑ Yes; ❑ No
Ceiling Fans	❑ Yes; ❑ No	❑ Yes; ❑ No	❑ Yes; ❑ No
Pool	❑ Yes; ❑ No	❑ Yes; ❑ No	❑ Yes; ❑ No
Recreation Room	❑ Yes; ❑ No	❑ Yes; ❑ No	❑ Yes; ❑ No
Onsite Laundry	❑ Yes; ❑ No	❑ Yes; ❑ No	❑ Yes; ❑ No
Onside Parking	❑ Yes; ❑ No	❑ Yes; ❑ No	❑ Yes; ❑ No
Notes			
Notes			
Notes			
Notes			
Notes			

Request for Credit Report

_____

_____

_____

Date: _____

RE: REQUEST FOR CREDIT REPORT

Dear _____,

I have recently had my Rental Application denied as a result of information contained on my credit report. Enclosed is a copy of that denial. Please send a copy of my credit report that was obtained as a part of my Rental Application. Please send it to my address at:

_____

_____

_____

_____

Sincerely,

Signature: _____

Printed Name: _____

Telephone: _____

Email: _____

Roommate Agreement

This Roommate Agreement is entered into by and between:

_____, "Roommate No. 1,"

_____, "Roommate No. 2,"

_____, "Roommate No. 3,"

_____, "Roommate No. 4", collectively "Roommates." This Roommate Agreement concerns the Lease Agreement for "Premises" located at: _____

_____

The Landlord is _____. The term of this Roommate Agreement will begin on the commencement date set forth in this Roommate Agreement and will end on the expiration date set forth in the Lease Agreement. This Roommate Agreement supersedes any oral or prior written agreement regarding roommate agreements. The Roommates acknowledge that no representation, inducements, promises, or agreements have been made by or on behalf of any party, except those covenants and agreements in this written agreement. Where context requires, the singular will include the plural, the plural the singular, and genders will include all genders. All Federal, State, and local laws apply where omitted. In consideration of the mutual promises, Roommates agree as follows:

1. **RIGHTS AND RESPONSIBILITIES.** This Roommate Agreement establishes the rights and responsibilities that the Roommates have with respect to each other. It does not replace or eliminate the rights and responsibilities arising from the Lease Agreement.

2. **RENT.** The rent of $ _____/ month is due on as specified in the Lease Agreement. Rent will be paid as follows:

   Roommate 1: $ _____   Roommate 2: $ _____

   Roommate 3: $ _____   Roommate 4: $ _____

   Roommate #: __ will pay the rent to the Landlord for the total month's rent and pay the Landlord on or before the first of each month according to the Lease Agreement. All other Roommates will pay their share to the Roommate paying the rent to the Landlord _____ days before the end of each month.

   The Roommates understand that if one or more of them does not pay his/her share of a utility bill, the other Roommate(s) must pay the unpaid share(s) or the utility may be discontinued. Each Roommate agrees that if other Roommate(s) pay his/her share of a utility bill, he/she will reimburse the other Roommate(s) as quickly as possible.

   Copies of all bills will be provided for inspection to any Roommate who makes a request. All bills will be kept in a safe place agreed upon by Roommate #: _____ to ensure they are available in the event of dispute.

3. **SECURITY DEPOSIT.** Each Roommate will pay an equal share of the Security Deposit proportionate to their share of the rent. Roommate #: _____ is responsible for collecting the Security Deposit and turning it into the Landlord.

4. **UTILITIES.** Each roommate will share equally the costs of: ❑ electricity, ❑ trash, ❑ sewer,

   ❑ gas, ❑ Internet, ❑ cable, ❑ landline phone,   ❑ _____

   ❑ _____   ❑ _____

   ❑ _____   ❑ _____

   Roommate #: _____ is responsible for collecting the utility payments from the other roommates and submitting the bills on time each month. All other Roommates will pay their share to the Roommate paying the utilities _____ days before the end of each month.

5. **COMMON AREAS.** Each Roommate will clean-up after themselves and not leave the common areas messy, including dirty dishes, food particles, or trash. Common areas that will be shared include: ❑ living room, ❑ kitchen, ❑ dining area, ❑ patio, ❑ bathroom,

   ❑ _____ ❑ _____ ❑ _____

   ❑ _____ ❑ _____ ❑ _____

6. **FOOD.** Each Roommate agrees to be responsible for his/her own food purchases and not to take food of the other Roommates without permission.

7. **CLEANING.** Each Roommate will clean his/her room and common areas after use. **No one will leave dishes in the sink for more than 24 hours, and everyone will promptly clean-up when asked.** The household chores for the rest of the common areas will rotate, with each Roommate responsible for vacuuming, dusting, and mopping on a weekly basis.

8. **GUESTS.** The Roommates agree to have no more than one overnight guest at a time following advance notice to the other Roommates, when possible. Each Roommate agrees to limit the number of overnight guests of each Roommate to no more than _____ guests   per month.

9. **JOINT AND SEVERAL LIABILITY.** Except as expressly stated in this Roommate Agreement (and prohibited by local laws), the Roommates agree that each Roommate is jointly and severally liable for all duties and obligations under the Lease Agreement, including the full rental amount as set out in the Lease Agreement, late fees, and breaches of contract.

10. **BREACHES AND VIOLATIONS OF THIS AGREEMENT.** The Roommates agree that repeated and serious breaches and violations of one or more of these provisions will be grounds for any Roommate to ask the other Roommate to leave. If a Roommate is asked to leave, the leaving Roommate must leave within two weeks, with forfeiture of any outstanding pre-paid rent and utilities. Roommates agree to act in good faith in dealings.

    Any act, failure, or omission to pay rent or utilities by any one of the Roommates may result in late fees or costs. Roommates that have paid their portion of the rent and utilities agree that any and all costs associated with an act, failure, or omission to pay rent or utilities by any of the other Roommate will be paid by the Roommate who committed the act, failure, or omission. Any Roommate who did not cause the act, failure, or omission to pay rent or utilities but paid any costs associated with an act, failure, or omission to pay rent or utilities may fully recover from all Roommates who caused the costs due to their act, failure, omission to pay rent or utilities.

11. **EARLY TERMINATION.** If a Roommate wants to leave before the end of the Lease Agreement and/or this Roommate Agreement expires, he/she will give as much notice as possible, but not less than one calendar month. The Roommate who leaves early (voluntarily or involuntarily) will get his/her share of the Security Deposit returned after costs of unpaid rent, repairs, replacement, and cleaning attributable to the departing Roommate have been subtracted. Until an acceptable Roommate is found, the departing Roommate will not receive any portion of his/her share of the Security Deposit until the tenancy of the remaining Roommates is over and the Security Deposit is refunded, in whole or in part. The vacating Roommate will provide a forwarding address to the Roommates.

12. **DISPUTE RESOLUTION.** The Roommates agree to act reasonably in their dealings with each other and to refrain from any behavior, action, or inaction that they know or reasonably should know will interfere with the other Roommates' quiet enjoyment. The Roommates agree to discuss concerns frankly and in a timely manner, and to refrain from emotional outbursts. Should negotiations be necessary, all Roommates agree to negotiate in good faith. All Roommates agree to respect all property, privacy, and sleep schedules to comply with all reasonable requests whenever possible. If a dispute arises concerning this Roommate Agreement or any aspect of the shared living situation, the Roommates have the option to terminate the tenancy or initiate a lawsuit.

13. **COPIES.** Roommate #: _____ will make copies of this signed Roommate Agreement and provide copies for each of the other Roommates and will provide a copy to the Landlord in a timely manner. The distributing Roommate will retain the original wet signature copy and make the original available for inspection by any of the other Roommates upon request.

Comments: _____

_____

_____

_____

_____

_____

_____

_____

By signing, the Roommate confirms that he/she has received, reviewed, and understands this Agreement.

_____	_____	_____	_____
Roommate 1	Date	Roommate 2	Date
_____	_____	_____	_____
Roommate 3	Date	Roommate 4	Date

Request to Add Tenant to Lease Agreement

_____

_____

_____

Date: _____

RE: REQUEST TO ADD TENANT TO LEASE AGREEMENT

Dear _____,

I currently reside at _____

_____

under a Lease Agreement with remaining _____month(s). I am requesting the following person be added to the Lease Agreement:

    Name: _____ Occupation: _____

    Relationship: _____ Credit Score: _____

He/she will be happy to furnish any additional information. The reason I am making this request is because: _____

_____

_____

_____

_____

I will remain responsible for the Lease Agreement, including paying the rent. If you have any questions, I can be reached at the below contacts.

    Sincerely,

    Signature: _____

    Printed Name: _____

    Telephone: _____

    Email: _____

Request to Assign Lease Agreement

_____

_____

_____

Date: _____

RE: REQUEST TO ASSIGN LEASE AGREEMENT

Dear _____,

I currently reside at _____

_____

under a Lease Agreement with remaining _____ month(s). I am requesting the assignment of the Lease Agreement, from _____ to _____, to the following person:

    Name: _____ Occupation: _____

    Relationship: _____ Credit Score: _____

He/she will be happy to furnish any additional information. The reason I am making this request is because: _____

_____

_____

_____

_____

If you have any questions, I can be reached at the below contacts.

    Sincerely,

    Signature: _____

    Printed Name: _____

    Telephone: _____

    Email: _____

Assignment of Lease Agreement

This Assignment of Lease Agreement ("Assignment Agreement") is entered into by and between:

_____, "Assignor,"

_____, "Assignee,"

collectively the "Parties." This Assignment Agreement concerns the Lease Agreement for the "Premises" located at: _____

_____

This Assignment Agreement supersedes any oral or prior written agreement regarding assignments. The Parties acknowledge that no representation, inducements, promises, or agreements have been made by or on behalf of any party, except those covenants and agreements in this written agreement. Where context requires, the singular will include the plural, the plural the singular, and genders will include all genders. All Federal, State, and local laws apply where omitted. In consideration of the mutual promises, the receipt and sufficiency of which is hereby acknowledged, the Parties agree to keep, perform and fulfill the promises, conditions and agreements below:

1. **ASSIGNED LEASE.** The Assignor assigns and transfers to the Assignee all of the Assignor's right, title, and interest in and to the Lease Agreement and the Premises, subject to all the conditions and terms contained therein.

2. **EFFECTIVE DATE.** This Assignment begins on _____ (the "Effective Date"), and continues until the present term of the Lease Agreement expires or on:

   _____, whichever occurs first.

3. **ASSIGNOR'S INTEREST.** The Assignor covenants that:

   a. the Assignor is the lawful and sole owner of the interest assigned under this Assignment;

   b. this interest is free from all encumbrances; and

   c. the Assignor has performed all duties and obligations and made all payments required under the Lease Agreement.

4. **BREACH OF LEASE BY ASSIGNEE.** In the event of a breach by the Assignee, the Landlord will provide the Assignor with written notice of this breach and the Assignor will have full rights to commence all actions to recover possession of the Premises (in the name of the Landlord, if necessary) and retain all rights for the duration of the Lease Agreement provided the Assignor will pay all accrued rents and cure any other default.

5. **GOVERNING LAW.** This Assignment is governed, to the exclusion of the law of any other forums, by the laws of the State of _____, without regard to the jurisdiction in which any action or special proceeding may be instituted.

6. **LEASE AGREEMENT.** This Assignment incorporates and is subject to the Lease Agreement, a copy of which is attached, and which is hereby referred to and incorporated as if it were set out here at length. The Assignee agrees to assume all of the obligations and responsibilities of

the Assignor under the Lease Agreement.

7. **TERMINATION OF LEASE AGREEMENT.** If Assignor terminates the Lease Agreement to the Premises, Assignor will provide thirty (30) days' notice to Assignee. Assignee agrees that if the Lease Agreement is terminated for any reason, this Assignment of Lease Agreement will terminate on the same date.

8. **BINDING AGREEMENT.** This Assignment will be binding on the Parties, their successors, assigns, personal representatives, beneficiaries, executors, administrators, and heirs, as applicable.

9. **ASSIGNEE'S DUTIES.** All rents and other charges accrued under the Lease Agreement prior to the Effective Date will be fully paid by the Assignor, and by the Assignee after the Effective Date. The Assignee will also be responsible for assuming and performing all other duties and obligations required under the terms and conditions of the Lease after the Effective Date.

10. **NOISE LEVEL.** During the hours of _____ to _____, the Assignee will maintain a noise level that will not reasonably disturb other persons.

11. **SMOKING.** Smoking is **NOT** allowed on the Premises.

12. **PARKING SPACE.** The Assignee agrees that Lessor ❑ is/ ❑ is not entitled to use a parking space as part of Assignment. The parking space, if any, is located at _____

_____

13. **DISPUTE RESOLUTION.** The Parties agree to act in good faith in their dealings with one another and to refrain from behavior, action, or inaction that they know, or reasonably should know, will interfere with the Premises condition. If a dispute arises from this Assignment, the Parties have the option to terminate the Assignment or initiate a lawsuit as permitted by law.

14. **FURTHER ASSIGNMENT.** There will be no further assignment of the Lease Agreement without the prior written consent of the Assignor.

Comments: _____

_____

_____

_____

_____

_____

_____

By signing below, Assignee confirms he/she has received, reviewed, and understands this Assignment.

_____   _____   _____   _____
Witness 1   Date   Witness 2   Date

_____   _____   _____   _____
Assignee   Date   Assignor   Date

Tenant Request to Sublease

_____

_____

_____

Date: _____

RE: REQUEST TO SUBLEASE

Dear _____,

I currently reside at _____

_____

under a Lease Agreement with remaining _____month(s). I am requesting to sublet the premises,

from _____ to _____, to the following person:

    Name: _____ Occupation: _____

    Relationship: _____ Credit Score: _____

He/she will be happy to furnish any additional information. The reason I am making this request is because: _____

_____

_____

_____

_____

If you have any questions, I can be reached at the below contacts.

    Sincerely,

    Signature: _____

    Printed Name: _____

    Telephone: _____

    Email: _____

Sublease Agreement

This Sublease Agreement is entered into by and between:

_____, "Lessor,"

_____, "Lessee,"

collectively the Parties. This Sublease Agreement concerns the Lease Agreement for the "Premises" located at: _____

_____

This Sublease Agreement supersedes any oral or prior written agreement regarding subleases. The Parties acknowledge that no representation, inducements, promises, or agreements have been made by or on behalf of any party, except those covenants and agreements in this written agreement. Where context requires, the singular will include the plural, the plural the singular, and genders will include all genders. All Federal, State, and local laws apply where omitted. In consideration of the mutual promises, Lessor agreeing to lease and the Lessee agreeing to assume the Lease for the Premises, and other valuable consideration, the receipt and sufficiency of which is hereby acknowledged, the Parties agree to keep, perform and fulfill the promises, conditions and agreements below:

The Lessor wishes to transfer to the Lessee the Lease Agreement dated _____

and executed by the Lessor as Tenant and by _____ as the "Landlord".

1. **SUBLEASE TERM.** The term of the Sublease will be for a period of _____ months, beginning on _____ and ending on _____. Lessee may share all of the common spaces (e.g., living room, dining room, kitchen, bathroom) in the Premises equally with the other Tenant(s), if any. The Lessee will limit the number of overnight guests to: _____ per night and no more than _____ nights per month of overnight guests. The Lessee ❑ does/ ❑ does not need to obtain Sublandlord's permission prior to the stay of any overnight guest(s).

2. **RENT.** Lessee will pay a total monthly rent of $_____. Rent will be payable on the first day of each month directly to the Lessor.

3. **SECURITY DEPOSIT.** Lessee will pay $_____ to Lessor as a Security Deposit. Deductions may be made from the Security Deposit and the remainder, if any, will be returned to Lessee within _____ days of the termination of Lessee's tenancy. The Security Deposit may not be used as last month's rent.

4. **UTILITIES.** The Lessee agrees to pay _____% of all utility charges.

5. **HOUSEHOLD CHORES.** The Tenants will divide all household chores as follows: _____

_____

_____

_____

6. **NOISE LEVEL.** During the hours of _____ to _____, the Lessee will maintain a noise level that will not reasonably disturb other persons.

7. **SMOKING.** Smoking is **NOT** allowed on the Premises.

8. **PARKING SPACE.** The Lessee agrees that Lessor ❑ is/ ❑ is not entitled to use a parking space as part of Assignment. The parking space, if any, is located at: _____

   _____

9. **LEASE AGREEMENT.** This Sublease incorporates and is subject to the Lease Agreement, a copy of which is attached, and which is hereby referred to and incorporated as if it were set out here at length. The Lessee agrees to assume all of the obligations and responsibilities of the Lessor under the Lease Agreement.

10. **TERMINATION OF LEASE AGREEMENT.** If Lessor terminates the Lease Agreement to the Premises, Lessor will provide thirty (30) days' notice to Lessee. Lessee agrees that if the Lease Agreement is terminated for any reason, this Sublease will terminate on the same date.

11. **CONDITION OF THE PREMISES.** Lessee acknowledges that he/she has examined the Premises and is in good condition except as follows _____

    _____

    Upon the termination of this Sublease Agreement, Lessee will vacate the Premises and leave it in its good condition on move-in. Lessee is responsible for the repair of any damage resulting from the act or neglect of Lessee or Lessee invitees.

12. **SUBLEASING AND ASSIGNMENT.** Lessee may not lease, sublease, or assign the Premises without the prior written consent of the Lessor.

13. **DISPUTE RESOLUTION.** The Parties agree to act in good faith in their dealings with one another and to refrain from behavior, action, or inaction that they know, or reasonably should know, will interfere with the Premises condition. If a dispute arises from this Sublease, the Parties have the option to terminate the Sublease or initiate a lawsuit as permitted by law.

Comments:_____

_____

_____

_____

By signing below, Lessee confirms that he/she has received, reviewed, and understands this Sublease.

_____	_____	_____	_____
Lessee	Date	Lessee	Date
_____	_____	_____	_____
Lessor	Date	Lessor	Date
_____	_____	_____	_____
Lessor Agent	Date	Lessor Agent	Date

House Sitting Agreement

This Housesitting Agreement is entered into by and between:

_____, "Home Owner,"

_____, "House Sitter,"

collectively the "Parties." This Housesitting Agreement concerns the "Premises" located at:

_____

_____

The term of this Housesitting Agreement will begin on the Commencement Date set forth in this Agreement and end on the Expiration Date also set forth in this Agreement. This Agreement supersedes any oral or prior written agreement regarding housesitting. The Parties acknowledge that no representation, inducements, promises, or agreements have been made by or on behalf of any party, except those covenants and agreements in this written agreement. Where context requires, the singular will include the plural, the plural the singular, and genders will include all genders. All Federal, State, and local laws apply where omitted. In consideration of the mutual promises, Home Owner gives House Sitter license to enter and occupy the Premises. The Parties agree to keep, perform, and fulfill the promises, conditions, and agreements below:

1. **TERMS AND CONDITIONS.** The Home Owner hereby gives the House Sitter license to enter and occupy the Premises beginning on: _____ ("Commencement Date") and ending on: _____ ("Expiration Date"). The House Sitter agrees to enter the Premises on the Commencement Date, to live in and occupy the Premises for the duration of this Agreement, and to vacate the Premises on the Expiration Date. The House Sitter may extend this Agreement with an advance notice of ten (10) calendar days.

2. **PETS.** The House Sitter's pets, if any, are permitted with prior written approval for the duration of this Agreement.

3. **OTHER OCCUPANTS.** The Parties agree that no person other than the House Sitter is permitted to live in or stay at the Premises during the term of this Agreement, unless otherwise agreed to by the Home Owner.

4. **RENT AND UTILITIES.** The Home Owner agrees to allow the House Sitter to occupy the Premises ❑ rent-free/ ❑ rent for $_____/ month for the term of this Agreement, in return for the care and upkeep of the Premises by the House Sitter. The Home Owner agrees to pay/ reimburse the House Sitter for the following costs and utilities:

   ❑ all costs incurred by the House Sitter in the care of the animals listed in this Agreement,

   ❑ electricity,

   ❑ gas,

   ❑ telephone landline, if any,

   ❑ water,

- ❏ Internet,

- ❏ Cable,

- ❏ Trash,

- ❏ Sewer,

- ❏ Waste removal charges.

5. **PREMISES CONDITION.** The Home Owner agrees to make sure the Premises are reasonably clean and fit for human habitation. The House Sitter agrees to take all reasonable steps in relation to the security, care and upkeep of the Premises, and to leave the Premises in a similar state of cleanliness and repair.

6. **URGENT REPAIRS.** The Home Owner agrees to pay, either directly to the service provider or as a reimbursement to the House Sitter, for the following urgent repairs:

- ❏ Burst water service;

- ❏ Blocked or broken lavatory system;

- ❏ Serious roof leak;

- ❏ Gas leak;

- ❏ Electrical faults;

- ❏ Flooding or serious flood damage;

- ❏ Serious storm damage;

- ❏ Serious fire damage;

- ❏ Failure or breakdown or the gas, electricity, or hot water to the Premises;

- ❏ Failure or breakdown of any essential service for hot water, cooking, heating or laundering;

- ❏ Any fault of damage that causes the Premises to be unsafe or not secure.

7. **REIMBURSEMENT.** Home Owner agrees to pay House Sitter, within seven (7) days of the end of this Agreement any reasonable costs House Sitter incurred for repairs to the Premises so long as:

   a. House Sitter was not in breach of this Agreement when the costs were incurred,

   b. House Sitter gives Home Owner a reasonable opportunity to make repairs,

   c. The repairs are carried out, where appropriate, by licensed or properly qualified persons, and

   d. House Sitter gives Home Owner written details of the repairs, including receipts for any costs that the House Sitter occurred.

8. **DISPUTE RESOLUTION.** In the event of a dispute, the Parties agree to negotiate in good faith. If a dispute arises concerning this Agreement, the Parties have the option to the Agreement

and initiate a lawsuit.

9. **HOUSE SITTER'S CONTACT DETAILS.** The Parties agree to provide their or their nominated contact person's contact details and to be readily contactable at all times. These details should remain current and functional for the term of this Agreement. The Parties can be contacted by the following methods:

Home Owner:

    a. Postal Address: _____

                          _____

                          _____

    b. Phone: _____

    c. E-mail: _____

House Sitter:

    a. Postal Address: _____

                          _____

                          _____

    b. Phone: _____

    c. E-mail: _____

Comments:_____

_____

_____

_____

_____

_____

_____

_____

_____

By signing below, the House Sitter acknowledges and confirms that he/she has received, reviewed, and understands this Housesitting Agreement.

_____	_____	_____	_____
House Sitter 1	Date	House Sitter 2	Date

_____	_____	_____	_____
Home Owner 1	Date	Home Owner 2	Date

Tenant Request to Extend Lease Agreement

_____

_____

_____

Date: _____

RE: REQUEST TO EXTEND LEASE AGREEMENT

Dear _____,

I currently reside at _____

_____

as your Tenant. I am requesting the Lease Agreement be extended until _____
with the same rate of rent.

The reason I am making this request is because: _____

_____

I hope this request meets with your approval, and I hope you will respond within **two weeks**. If you have
any questions, I can be reached at the below contacts. Thank you for your time and consideration.

     Sincerely,

     Signature: _____

     Printed Name: _____

     Telephone: _____

     Email: _____

Repair Request

_____

_____

_____

Date: _____

RE: REPAIR REQUEST

Dear _____,

I currently reside at _____

_____

as your Tenant. I am writing to inform you of the following problems that need to be repaired:

_____

_____

_____

_____

_____

_____

_____

_____

❑   I grant permission to the Landlord, Landlord's Agents, and/or sub-contractor(s) under the Landlord's direction to enter the Premises for the purpose of making the necessary repairs if I am not present.

If you have any questions, I can be reached at the below contacts.

    Sincerely,

    Signature: _____

    Printed Name: _____

    Telephone: _____

    Email: _____

Follow-Up Repair Request

_____

_____

_____

Date: _____

RE: FOLLOW-UP REPAIR REQUEST

Dear _____,

I currently reside at _____

_____

as your Tenant. In reference to my Repair Request Form dated _____, I am writing to follow-up on the status of my request for repairing the following:

_____

_____

_____

_____

_____

_____

_____

I am requesting that you take action within the next_____ days.

- ❑ I grant permission to the Landlord, Landlord's Agents, and/or sub-contractor(s) under the Landlord's direction to enter the Premises for the purpose of making the necessary repairs if I am not present.

If you have any questions, I can be reached at the below contacts.

Sincerely,

Signature: _____

Printed Name: _____

Telephone: _____

Email: _____

Notice of Insurance Claim Filed

_____

_____

_____

Date: _____

RE: INSURANCE CLAIM FILED

Dear _____,

I currently reside at _____

_____

as your Tenant. I am writing to inform you that I filed an insurance claim on: _____

The insurance claim was filed because: _____

_____

_____

_____

_____

_____

_____

_____

_____

_____

If you have any questions, I can be reached at the below contacts.

    Sincerely,

    Signature: _____

    Printed Name: _____

    Telephone: _____

    Email: _____

Compliant Letter to Landlord

_____

_____

_____

Date: _____

RE: COMPLIANT

Dear _____,

I currently reside at _____

_____

as your Tenant. I am writing because I have the following compliant:

_____

_____

_____

_____

This problem is affecting my enjoyment of the Premises for approximately the past _____ days. As you are aware when I spoke to you regarding this matter on _____. I am disappointed it has not yet been resolved. Specifically, I have documented the following:

_____

_____

Please take the following action(s) immediately: _____

_____

Please let me know when the matter will be addressed. I would appreciate a phone call following-up, as soon as possible.

    Sincerely,

    Signature: _____

    Printed Name: _____

    Telephone: _____

    Email: _____

Notice to Vacate

_____

_____

_____

Date: _____

RE: NOTICE TO VACATE

Dear _____,

I currently reside at _____

_____

as your Tenant. Pursuant to the Lease Agreement I am providing this as a written notice of my intent to vacate. My last day will be: _____.

❑   I wish to schedule a walk-through inspection of the Premises.

❑   I do <u>not</u> wish to schedule a walk-through inspection of the Premises.

I expect my full Security Deposit of $ _____ to be refunded to my address:

_____

_____

_____

_____

Should you have any issues or questions, please feel free to contact me. Thank you for your time.

    Sincerely,

    Signature: _____

    Printed Name: _____

    Telephone: _____

    Email: _____

Demand Letter for Security Deposit

_____

_____

_____

Date: _____

RE: DEMAND LETTER FOR SECURITY DEPOSIT

Dear _____,

I currently reside at _____

_____

Following my 30-day written Notice to Vacate, I moved out leaving the Premises cleaner than when I moved in. In addition, my rent was fully up-to-date by the time I left the Premises, and I gave you a forwarding address. I have not yet received the $_____ Security Deposit or an itemized statement documenting any deductions for the Security Deposit. The Security Deposit is _____ days late.

I am sending this formal Demand Letter in the hopes of resolving this matter quickly. Please be aware that I know about my rights under the law. If I do not receive the Security Deposit by: _____ I have the right to take this matter to small claims court. If I am compelled to take this matter to small claims court, I will sue for the full Security Deposit amount plus punitive damages allowed under State law. Please send my Security Deposit immediately. Should you have any issues or questions, please contact me.

Sincerely,

Signature: _____

Printed Name: _____

Telephone: _____

Email: _____

Address: _____

_____

_____

_____

Second Demand Letter for Security Deposit

_____

_____

_____

Date: _____

RE: SECOND DEMAND LETTER FOR SECURITY DEPOSIT

Dear _____,

I am writing to return the Security Deposit I made for Premises leased at: _____

_____

On _____ I sent you a written Demand Letter for the return of my Security Deposit. To this date, I have not received the $ _____ Security Deposit or an itemized statement documenting any deductions for the Security Deposit. The Security Deposit is over _____ days late. Following my 30-day written Notice to Vacate, I moved out leaving the Premises cleaner than when I moved in. In addition, my rent was fully up-to-date when I left, and I gave you a forwarding address. This is my second, and final attempt, to resolve this matter without small claims court.

As I mentioned in the previous Demand Letter, I am aware of my rights under the law. If I do not receive the Security Deposit by: _____ I will begin the process of taking this matter to small claims court. This second demand letter, as well as the first demand letter, may be used to show that I have acted in good faith to seek the return of the Security Deposit. If I am compelled to take this matter to court, I will sue for the full Security Deposit plus punitive damages allowed under State law. Please send my Security Deposit immediately.

Sincerely,

Signature: _____

Printed Name: _____

Telephone: _____

Email: _____

Address: _____

_____

_____

_____

Tenant Dispute of Security Deposit Itemization

This is a request to return the full Security Deposit I made for Premises leased located at: _____

_____

as your Tenant. To this date, I have not received the $ _____ Security Deposit.
I dispute the Itemized Security Deposit Statement documenting the deductions from the Security Deposit.
I dispute the following deductions that were itemized when you returned a portion/failed to return my
Security Deposit:

Itemized Deduction	Dispute Reason:

Please send my full Security Deposit immediately to the address below. Should you have any issues or
questions, please feel free to contact me.

Sincerely,

Signature: _____

Printed Name: _____

Telephone: _____

Email: _____

Address: _____

_____

_____

_____

VII. You Created Your Legal Documents, Now What?

A.   Storing Documents

Now that you have created your legal documents, you need to store them. You will also need to know how to make changes. In this chapter, you will learn how to store and make changes to your legal documents.

1.   Where to Keep It

Copies are generally provided by the Landlord. The Landlord and Tenant each keep a signed copy of the documents with the Landlord retaining the original wet signature copies. Legal documents should be easy to find and stored where they will not get damaged by accidents or the elements. Knowledge of the location of legal documents should be limited to a need to know basis. While secrecy may not be required, confidential information is located in the documents and efforts should be made to protect privacy. Properly storing documents is very important.

Generally, people store all of their legal documents together in a folder or scanned onto a computer drive. These are all excellent places to store your legal documents because they can be easily accessible to you, but more difficult for guests and invitees who may accidently discover the documents.

There is no legal requirement for where you should store your legal documents. That is entirely up to you.

2.   How to Keep It

When you store your legal documents, you can staple the pages together along with any addendums, attachments, and/or any other documents that you want to keep together. You may want to put your documents in reverse chronological order with the most recent documents on-top. As general practice, keeping your legal documents together helps identify what has been agreed with changes over time.

3. Making Copies

Copying your legal documents is practical. Copies can generally be used in court, and they are generally permissible so long as there are no questions as to their authenticity or completeness. The copies should be complete and accurately representations of the original. Check your local jurisdictions for specifics. Landlords should keep original wet signature copies as well as make copies for tenants. All copies should be clearly legible, especially regarding dates and money.

B.   Making Changes to   Existing Documents

Changes are permitted and can be achieved through subsequent agreements between the parties.

Most jurisdictions follow the principle of last in time i.e., where there are similar provision or documents that are conflicting, the one created last in time will prevail. There may be small differences based on your circumstances (it would be wise to consult a lawyer on such matters).

1.   How to Make Changes

Changes to your legal documents, made after the documents have been signed can be done by including a statement that supersedes all prior documents. This statement must be signed by all the parties and dated. A statement that you put in your new legal documents that supersedes the previous one is known as a *codicil* or an *amendment*. Generally, it is best to add a codicil that rejects all prior documents and makes your changes in a new document. A good general practice is to enter into a completely new agreement rather than continuously add codicils because overtime it can be difficult to track what changes are made whereas if an entirely new document is created then the last document created will likely control.

2.   Consequences of Not Making Changes

Failure to change your documents after significant changes are required can have unintended consequences. For example, local laws may only allow rent to increase for certain types of properties at a certain percentage and after proper notice. If you do not make changes to your documents then the rent may be lower than what you would want from the property. You will also have to spend the added cost of resolving disputes that were not addressed elsewhere but could have been added later in time.

3.   Ending a Legal Document

For a lease agreement to end at the completion of the terms agreed requires very little. As a landlord, you can either send out an offer to extend a lease or you can inform the tenant that at the end of the lease agreement the tenant will need to vacate. If a tenant does not want to extend, the tenant will need to inform the landlord. Once the landlord knows the future of the current tenant, the landlord can act accordingly.

If you want to end a lease agreement before the natural end of the lease agreement, you generally need cause. If the tenant violates the lease agreement or fails to pay rent, you may very well be able to end the lease agreement.   To end a lease agreement under these circumstances generally requires documenting bad acts. Other options include paying the tenant to vacate.

Unilaterally changing documents or imposing unreasonable conditions of tenants is generally not going to be acceptable. In addition, you cannot end an agreement simply by physical action such as tearing the lease agreement, scratching out signatures, or in some other way, physically destroying the documents. Physically destroying any of the legal documents will have no effect on their legality. To revoke these legal documents, you will need to enter into a separate codicil that revokes the documents.

4.   Reviving a Revoked Legal Document

When you end an agreement, either because it reached its term end or by codicil, you cannot generally revive the agreement simply by oral agreement or by a unilateral notice to tenant that the previous agreement that ended is being revived. It is bad practice to try to do so. You and the tenants will need to enter into the exact same written agreement again with new signatures and dates. No prior versions of legal document are revived automatically. To revive an earlier version, you would need to create a new document that contains your needs. You can make adjustments as needed and do not need to be mirror images of the previous agreement.

5.   If a Legal Document Is Missing

If the original legal document cannot be found, courts will generally allow copies so long as the parties agree that the copies provided are complete and accurate representations of the original. If there are questions as to which documents are the correct representations, courts will look to the parties or may create their own version of what the agreement were that may or may not favor your side. Therefore, it is important to properly store documents.

VIII. Additional Resources

A.   Attorneys

While you are creating your legal documents, or even after you have created them, you may need additional resource. In this chapter, you will learn about retaining an attorney.

1.   Hiring an Attorney

If you think you can simply complete the sample forms in this book and have an attorney look them over for you, you may have a hard time finding an attorney that will take on the job. Even if you do find an attorney willing to take it on, you may find it to be more costly than having them create the documents. One reason may be the attorney may not be comfortable taking on someone else's work on their reputation. If you decide to hire an attorney, there are some things to consider, including the type of attorney, finding an attorney, and fees.

2.   Type of an Attorney to Hire

The type of attorney that you hire depends on what problem you need to solve. For landlord-tenant law, you may need an attorney who specializes in real estate or property law as well as contracts, tax, or business law. Your attorney, at a minimum, should be a member a State's bar association. You should seek an attorney with whom you feel comfortable talking because the information that you provide is likely personal in nature.

3.   Finding an Attorney

There are many ways to go about finding a competent attorney. You can ask family, friends, or businesses that you respect for recommendations. Generally, you can go to an attorney that you have been referred to even if they do not practice in landlord-tenant, real estate, or property law. They may take you as a client, or they may refer you to someone else. You can search online on an established online directory that allows you to narrow your search by location and practice area. However, these directories tend to list established attorneys with high fees. If you are part of a group legal plan as part of a union, employer, or consumer group, you might start with them and get your problems taken care of for free or at a reduced rate.

4.   Attorney Fees

Attorneys can be expensive. Fees commonly range from $150 to $500 per hour, or more. But higher rates do not always translate into better service. You may be better-off with an attorney that understands your unique situation. Fees should be disclosed upfront, and you should make sure to get something affirmative in writing. If you agree to a set price for the work to be completed, you should know if and what conditions can change, such as the hourly rate.

B.   Legal Research

Doing your own legal research is a challenge because you may not know where to even go to look for resources. Even when you find information, you may not know if the information you are finding is correct, relevant, or up-to-date. For these reasons, and more, we do not recommend that you rely solely on your own legal research or one source of information.

1.   Libraries

Going to a law library and searching online can serve as a useful starting point. Most law school libraries are Federal repositories and are open to the public during normal business hours. While at the law library, librarians are usually happy to help you find information and provide you with some guidance about where to begin your research. Some public libraries have a small collection of legal self-help books that may be useful research tools. In addition, your local county courthouse may have a law library, selections vary.

2.   Online

It is possible to find quality information online. You personally have to gauge, not only the reputation of the information that you are being presented, but also the date of the information. If you go to a law library, a librarian may recommend some online tools as well as some printed materials.

Please consider reviewing our book on Amazon.com or elsewhere. Visit PeerlessLegal.com.
Other titles by Peerless Legal include:

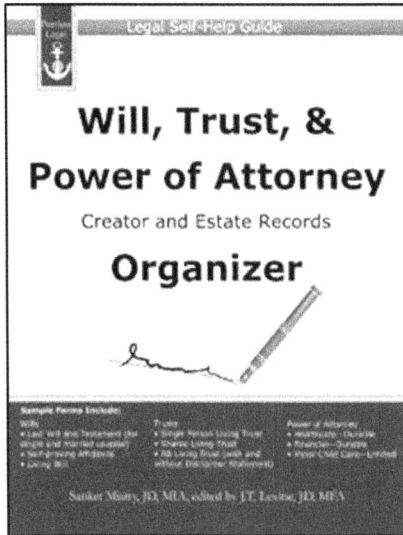
Legal Self-Help Guide
Will, Trust, & Power of Attorney
Creator and Estate Records
Organizer
Sanket Mistry, JD, MIA, edited by J.T. Levine, JD, MFA

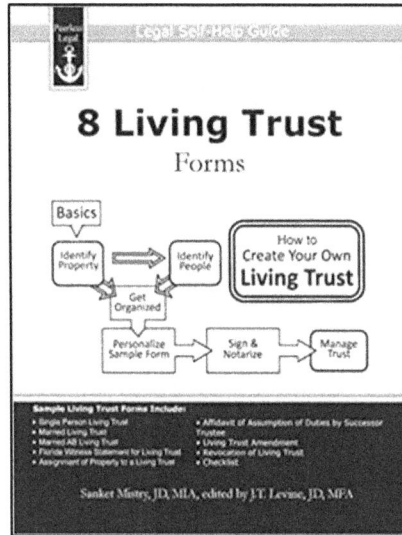
Legal Self-Help Guide
8 Living Trust
Forms
Sanket Mistry, JD, MIA, edited by J.T. Levine, JD, MFA

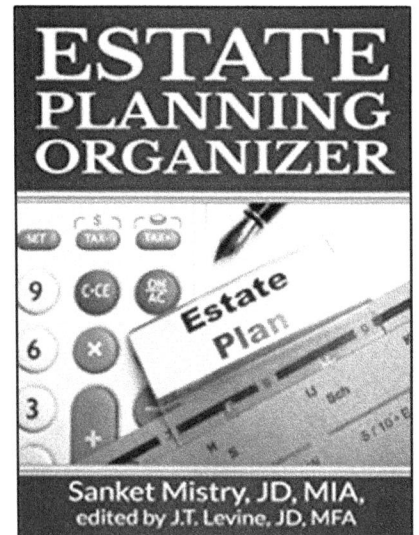
ESTATE PLANNING ORGANIZER
Estate Plan
Sanket Mistry, JD, MIA, edited by J.T. Levine, JD, MFA

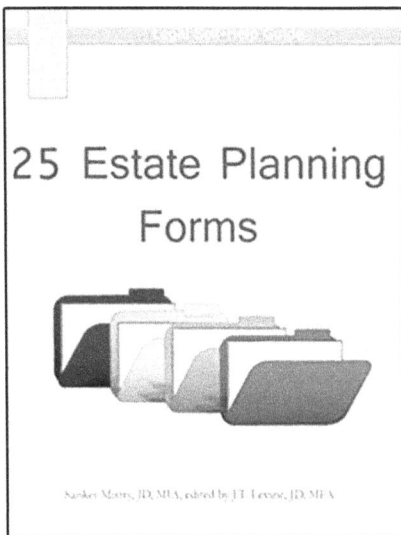
25 Estate Planning Forms
Sanket Mistry, JD, MIA, edited by J.T. Levine, JD, MFA

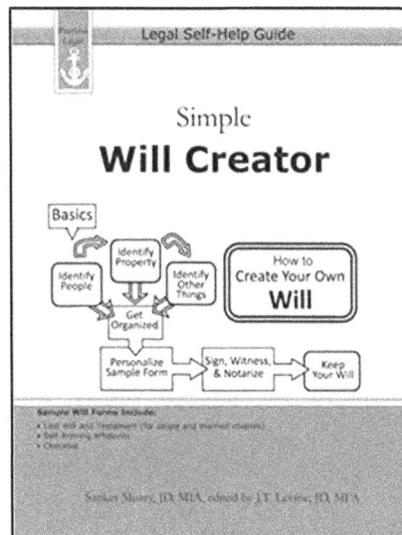
Legal Self-Help Guide
Simple
Will Creator
Sanket Mistry, JD, MIA, edited by J.T. Levine, JD, MFA

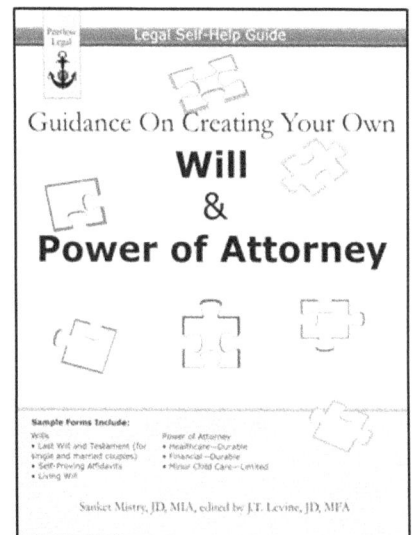
Legal Self-Help Guide
Guidance On Creating Your Own
Will & Power of Attorney
Sanket Mistry, JD, MIA, edited by J.T. Levine, JD, MFA

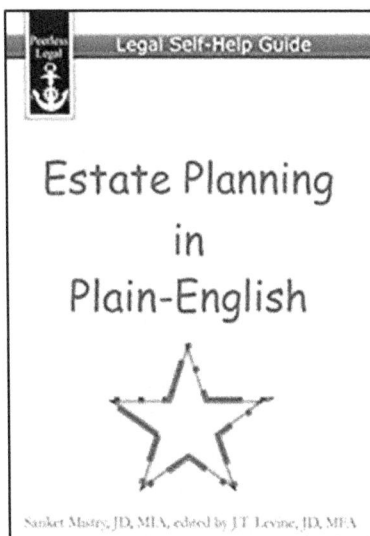
Legal Self-Help Guide
Estate Planning in Plain-English
Sanket Mistry, JD, MIA, edited by J.T. Levine, JD, MFA

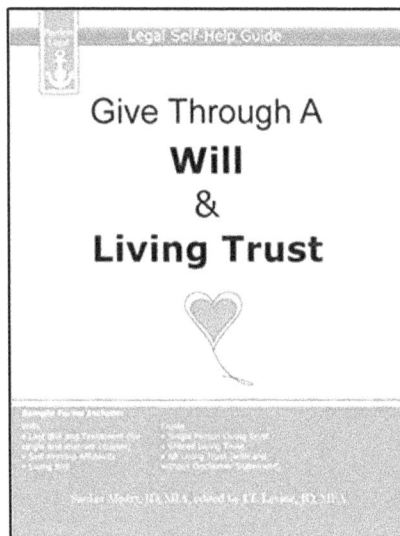
Legal Self-Help Guide
Give Through A
Will & Living Trust
Sanket Mistry, JD, MIA, edited by J.T. Levine, JD, MFA